FIT
FOR
FREEDOM

H. Philip Constans, Jr.
Western Kentucky University

University Press
of America™

"Stubborn Ounces" is reprinted from *SIGNATURE, New and Selected Poems* by Bonard W. Overstreet, with the permission of W. W. Norton and Company, Inc. Copyright © 1978 by W. W. Norton and Company, Inc.

Library of Congress Catalog Card Number: 79-6405

To Socrates

and Bruno

and John Scopes

and Barbara Franklin

and Willa Johnson

and Hal Lewis.

To George Dabbs

and Michael Littleford

and Kathy McDevitt

and Joe Ward

and Jim Hilliard.

To Charles Black

and Tom Carroll

and .....

and the several thousand teachers who,
like these, have had the courage.

And, to the several hundred thousand teachers who will
somehow find the courage to get this job done.

iii

Fit For Freedom

Preface

The purpose of this book is to set forth a plan by which the public schools of the United States of America can produce a person who will function as a responsible citizen in our form of democracy--a person who is fit for freedom. No, this isn't one more Civics book or even a book about political socialization. It's the outline of a comprehensive total school program for citizenship education. To establish the need for such a program as this will, of course, require the development of some foundational understandings.

Even a casual reading for a week of any but the most provincial newspaper or the viewing of a week's worth of the nightly news will clearly establish that we have a serious citizenship problem in the United States of America. It is simple enough to "view with alarm" the easily assembled signs of citizen impotence, apathy, and ignorance. Over and over again we see the evidence of government by special interest. Each day brings another account of the incredible gullibility and tolerance of corruption that is the hallmark of the American citizen.

On the day that I am writing these words, the local newspapers feature a story of one of our Kentucky congressmen pocketing fifteen thousand dollars from his "stationery" account while others of our Kentucky representatives withdrew amounts of $3,000., $6,584.79, $3,000. and $3,400. On this day I also find a headline that says "Goldwater denies mob ties," and an article in which an aide to our Governor explains that the head of our state really wasn't "ripping us off" when he had a Lincoln Continental limousine driven to Washington for his use while he attended a Governor's conference and stayed in a $230. a day hotel suite.

Many is the political career that has been successfully built on the assumption that the citizenry

iv

is stupid, self-centered, immature, and lazy. Truly any week's news will provide a prophet of doom with an abundance of material for the prediction of the decline and fall of the American democracy. While I do not share such a gloomy view of our future, I recognize that we have a constant supply of irrefutable evidence that we have a very serious problem. It is the existence of this problem that establishes the need for this book. In various portions of this book I will deal in detail with some of the specific dimensions of this problem as they relate to particular points that I am making. However, the existence of the problem is obvious and I will not cite every minute scrap of relevant evidence that might be assembled. It is to solve this problem that I have developed the program of education that this book contains. Starting then from the assumption that there is a serious citizenship problem, I will seek to establish an understanding of three primary concepts on which I base the educational program I propose.

First, I will seek to establish that a relationship exists between freedom, as I understand it, and a form of government that is known as representative democracy.

Second, I will undertake to establish beyond any doubt that the production of responsible citizens is the job of public education. While this ought to go without saying, there is some reason to believe that, beyond the verbal level, there is little real acceptance or understanding of this responsibility. In this regard I want to at least deal with the topic to the extent that I make it clear that the standard "cop out" of blaming the parents is not applicable here and to clearly establish that a responsible citizenry is the job of public education. Further, I want to make it plain that this is the job of all public education and not just the social studies teachers.

Third, I want to make clear what I'm talking about when I refer to responsible citizenship in a democracy. I am painfully aware that the business of defining terms has from time to time become an obsession that has tended to immobilize thinking. I truly don't want to get caught in that trap. On the other hand, I do want to detail the definition I am using in discussing responsible citizenship at least to the point that, agree or not, you will know how I'm using the concept.

Thus, when I write about a responsible citizen being one who understands our system of government, stays informed, thinks critically, participates actively, and accepts the basic tenets of democracy, it will be for the purpose of making clear what I am talking about.

Having established the framework within which I am operating, I want to take a hard look at how well we in public education are doing the job of producing responsible citizens. Now, this is not one of those "America is going to hell in a wheelbarrow" books. Neither is it a book that contends the "public schools are a total failure and should be scrapped." On the contrary, in this portion of the book I will try to make a very realistic and hard-nosed appraisal of the degree of both the success and the failures we public school teachers have had in citizenship education. This appraisal will no doubt be colored by my own great affection for this country, my deep commitment to what I understand to be the basic tenets of democracy, and my tremendous admiration for the public schools of the United States of America. In this latter connection I am not among those who stand aghast at the failures of public education but rather among those who are amazed at the remarkable amount of success that public school teachers have achieved in the face of almost insurmountable obstacles. On the other hand, I trust that this great reservoir of appreciation will in no way keep me from seeing fault where fault lies and failure where it exists. No institution or individual ever improved through ignoring its own shortcomings.

Next, and this is the major thrust of the book, I want to describe the way schools will be if we are to have an educational system that is in fact effective in the production of responsible citizens. In this portion of the book I will deal with the kinds of things kids should learn. Not just those basic understandings of the philosophy, history, tradition, structure, and mechanics of democratic government but the realities of government as it presently operates in America. Further, I will deal with the teaching of skills that a citizen in a democracy must have available to him, such as logic, critical thinking, propaganda analysis, effective communication, and systematic decision making.

Not only do I suggest that these skills be learned but that a systematic program be developed that will provide children with experience in using them in both simulated and real life situations. Finally, I will give attention to the importance of deliberately structuring the environment of the schools so as to support and promote the development of attitudes and values that are essential to responsible democratic citizenship. In this regard I will address my attention to the significance of the examples set by teachers, the need to alter the basic approach that schools take toward children, the need for schools to redefine their concept of "good citizenship," and the necessity of a complete reorganization of the administrative structure of the schools. It is not my intention to get into the specific details of particular courses and units, as this is most certainly not intended as a "methods" book. What I do want to do is give a comprehensive picture of what a school system that is serious about producing responsible citizens will be like.

Finally, I want to take measure of the practicality of my proposals. It is easy enough to set forth a utopian plan by which all that is wrong can be righted. It is quite another thing to consider proposals in the light of reality to ascertain if they can actually be put into practice in public education.

I believe it is customary in a preface to give a listing of those for whom the book is intended--sort of a catalog of suggested users. This book is aimed at school teachers and those who plan to be school teachers. Beyond this, I am convinced that there is a desperate need for such a book. If I'm correct in this assumption, perhaps a greater audience will find the book without my drawing a map.

My major concern in writing is to communicate my ideas. Far too often college professors write to impress their colleagues with their "scholarliness." Such endeavors are too often exercises in the fine art of obfuscation. I'll try hard to avoid obscuring the obvious, complicating the simple or lengthening the short. If I err, it is my fondest hope that it will be in the direction of plain speaking. I hope this book will be interesting. More important, I hope it will move you to action.

To those who have been of help to me in this undertaking, I thank you.

TABLE OF CONTENTS

PREFACE iv

PART I - THE FOUNDATION

Chapter 1 - Freedom. 2

Chapter 2 - Whose Business?. 7

Chapter 3 - A Responsible Citizen Is... 12

     Summary. 16

PART II - HOW ARE WE DOING?

Chapter 4 - He Understands 18

Chapter 5 - He Supports. 33

Chapter 6 - He Stays Informed. 44

Chapter 7 - He Thinks Critically 52

Chapter 8 - He Participates. 62

     Summary. 65

PART III - WHAT'S WRONG?

Chapter 9 - Is It Possible?. 68

Chapter 10 - Why Hasn't It Happened?. 75

PART IV - WHAT TO DO

Chapter 11 - The Theory 82

Chapter 12 - The Knowledge. 90

Chapter 13 - The Skills 98

Chapter 14 - The Attitude Through Environment . . . 108

Chapter 15 - The Attitude Through Example 120

Chapter 16 - Reality. 129

PART I

THE FOUNDATION

FREEDOM

This book is about democracy, about education, and about the necessary relationship of one to the other. It occurred to me to entitle it <u>Democracy</u> <u>and</u> <u>Education</u>, Part II. Fortunately, discretion won a close battle over crass opportunism and I settled on the title <u>Fit</u> <u>For</u> <u>Freedom</u>.

There are some purists that contend that freedom cannot be contingent--that you have it without any limitations, conditions, requirements or responsibilities, or you don't have it at all. In theory this may sound good. But such a definition, while perhaps nice to contemplate, holds out to man, the social being, a definition of freedom that is meaningless and unattainable. In the social setting in which humankind inevitably finds itself, such a concept is more likely described as license, while freedom becomes identified with both limitations, conditions and responsibilities. It is in this latter sense that the term will be used in this book. Thus, as used here, it is a relative concept that is both limited and contingent. Freedom is limited in the day-to-day world of human contact by the legitimate rights of other human beings. Freedom is contingent on its exercise for its continuation. While it may or may not be the natural order of things, freedoms that are not used tend to cease to exist. It is the exercise of freedom that appears to keep it alive and this, the exercise of freedom, then becomes the responsibility of one who intends to stay free.

Such being the case, if one is to maintain his freedom, within the limits noted above, there are things he must do. In this sense, it is the person who not only knows what to do and how to do it, but also practices those things he knows, who is "fit for freedom."

Obviously the concept of conditional freedom that I am using places great value on human dignity and worth.

I have at least a nodding acquaintance with the works of those who contend that the full development of

2

man through social engineering is deterred by such humanistic concepts as freedom and dignity. I've even forced myself to trudge through the pages of B.F. Skinners' Beyond Freedom and Dignity. In truth, I believe that this behavioristic concept of man is folderol, which is the academic equivalent of "hogwash." Since the beginning of education we have tried in one form or another to develop human beings through habituation, or "operant conditioning," if you please. It hasn't worked and it's not going to work. It hasn't worked and it's not going to work because it is contrary to what history teaches us about human beings. There seems to be some sort of life force within humans that causes them to be more than just the sum of their experiences--more than just a series of responses to stimuli. With the possible exception of Sartre (perhaps) every philosopher of stature with whom I am familiar recognizes either implicitly or explicitly this life force. You can easily think of this force, or as Bergson calls it the elan vital,* as that which gives man dignity and the pressure that, weak or strong, ceaselessly nudges him toward freedom. In any event, it surely is the force that has from the beginning of education caused our attempts to habituate to meet so little success. I'll have more to say about this later in the book. It is at the point of valuing human dignity and worth that the concept of democracy enters in, for among the political arrangements developed by man, democracy places great value on the individual human being. To the extent that the nurturing of effective democracy contributes to the maintenance of individual freedom, one can assume that that which promotes one also promotes the other. In other words, I view the political arrangement known as democracy as a means, perhaps the best means, by which individual freedom can be enhanced. Such being the case, it follows that one who functions as an effective and responsible citizen in a democracy is doing those things that render him "fit for freedom."

Since it must be done sometime, I suppose that this is as good a place as any to pause and deal with the differing concepts of democracy. Let's start first with the "purists" who insist that it is wrong to even refer to the government of the United States of America as a democracy. To them, one who fails to label our government a "republic" is at best ignorant,

---

* I just threw this elan vital bit in to add a little tone.

and at worst part of some deep dark conspiracy that is out to do us in. To these good folks, I respond, "piffle," which is roughly the academic equivalent of "nuts." This may appear to be giving short shrift to those who have labored long in the vineyards of super patriotism, and it is. It is the cavalier treatment that one deserves who insists on such pickiness in an effort to claim sole province over the subject matter. The Greek root words of Democracy are <u>Demos</u>, the common people; and <u>kratia</u>, power. The theoretical basis of our form of government is that the people rule or have power, and that means Democracy. So much for the purists.

There are, of course, several forms of democracy with a major division occurring between direct participation and indirect. Obviously our form of democracy falls within the indirect category. Further, within the indirect form of democracy there are several types. The distinction between these several types deserves some consideration. In his book, <u>Political Learning</u>, <u>Political</u> Choice, and <u>Democratic Citizenship</u>, Robert Weissberg discusses three concepts of indirect democracy.[1] He writes of participatory democracy, representative democracy and electoral competetion democracy. In participatory democracy, which really borders on direct democracy, the political process permeates every aspect of the lives of the people, and they have a voice in all matters that affect any part of their lives. Such a concept is not limited to government but is much broader and can be said to be realized when people are effectively in control of their own lives. On the other hand, representative democracy is a more narrow concept in that it is limited to control of the government. Representative democracy incorporates two major concepts. First, it requires an informed electorate that selects leaders who are responsive to public opinion. Second, there are several basic freedoms that must be available to all citizens. The electoral competition variety of democracy is based on the single premise that the citizens have the right to choose their leaders in competitive elections. If this later concept is to be accepted as a form of democracy at all, it must be placed in the bare bones, irreducible minimal category.

---

[1]Robert Weissberg, <u>Political Learning</u>, <u>Political Choice</u>, and <u>Democratic Citizenship</u>, Englewood Cliffs, N.J., Prentice Hall, 1974, pp. 174-182.

Obviously, because I am concerned with and committed to the maintenance of human freedom, any concept of democracy that views basic freedoms as non-essential falls short of that which I consider to be adequate. For this reason, if for no other, the concept of electoral competitive democracy will not be used in this book as the definition of democracy or basis for determining responsible democratic citizenship. At the other end of the spectrum, to the extent that participatory democracy isn't another term for anarchy, it is most certainly a laudable but presently unattainable ideal. Perhaps should the time come when we learn to effectively exercise control over our own government, it will then become practical to move beyond to effective control over every aspect of our lives. In the interim, I'll hold in abeyance the idea of participatory democracy and settle for the awesome task of trying to set forth a workable program for the development of citizens who can, and will make representative democracy work.

It will, then, be on the basis of representative democracy that I will define responsible citizenship and develop my ideas about how to produce such citizens. More specifically, the representative democracy to which I will be referring includes the following basic premises:

(1) That Government must be by the consent of the governed. This premise includes the right of the electorate to expect those who represent them to be responsive to the wishes and needs of the majority.

(2) That an enlightened electorate is required. Such a premise assumes a citizenry that has both the skills and the information necessary for making decisions about matters of government.

(3) That government must protect certain basic human rights. Certainly to be included among these is freedom of speech and association, equal protection under the law, freedom of assembly, the right to petition for redress of grievances, and the freedom of access to information on matters about which the citizen must make decisions.

The premises of representative democracy will hardly prove shocking or unfamiliar to anyone with even

WHOSE BUSINESS?

What I want to do in this chapter is establish beyond a doubt the fact that the production of responsible citizens for the American form of representative democracy is the business of the public schools. I'm being emphatic about this because it has been my experience that at a vague generalized level the most customary response is, "So, what's new. Everybody knows that." Yet, more often than not, when this topic becomes specific and direct questions about responsibility need to be answered, the general agreement disappears.

History teaches us that social orders try to perpetuate themselves. Over and over again when a particular group has come to power in a society, they have gone to great lengths to see that the "proper" order of things, as they see it, is continued into the future. Obviously, to do this they must somehow try to exercise control over the future. The future of any society is, of course, in its youth. Therefore--and this is so obvious and trite that I blush to commit it to writing--if a society is going to successfully perpetuate itself it must control its future by effectively influencing its young. Over and over again societies have sought to do this through some means of formal education or schooling. Now, there may well be other reasons why societies establish schools but without question one of the reasons--in all likelihood the major reason--is the perpetuation of that society.

Look at your history. While it has frequently been the philosophers who have sought to have their ideas translated into the reality of the future through advocating a particular kind of education, it has been those in control of a social order who have actually done this so as to perpetuate their society. This schooling didn't necessarily mean mass education, as this wasn't terribly necessary if you only needed to educate a few to rule.

Look to the early days of what is now the

Roman Catholic Church and see the establishment of an educational system that continues today for the purpose of perpetuating that particular order of things. Look into antiquity and see the schools of the Hebrews, the Indians, the Chinese and you will discover that this was their purpose. Look at the haste with which Adolph Hitler grabbed the schools of Germany so as to insure that the Third Reich would last a thousand years. Look at the history of our own country. Look to Massachusetts where this colony established mass education so that the Bible could be read, in that Bible-based social order, so that their children would not be deluded and led astray by Satan. Societies set up schools to perpetuate themselves. The schools are intended to perpetuate that society by producing "responsible citizens" for it. Depending on the time and particular social order, schools of a society may very well have other functions, but these in no wise reduce the obligation to produce responsible citizens.

Listen to the words of our founding fathers:

"If a nation expects to remain ignorant and free in a state of civilization, it expects what never was and never will be."

Thomas Jefferson

"Promote, then as an object of primary importance, institutions for the general diffusion of knowledge. In proportion as the structure of government gives force to public opinion, it is essential that public opinion should be enlightened."

George Washington

"To confirm the principles, morals and manners of our citizens to our republican forms of government, it is absolutely necessary that knowledge of every kind should be disseminated through every part of the United States."

Benjamin Rush

"Knowledge will forever govern ignorance; and a people who mean to be their own governors must arm themselves with the power which knowledge gives. "

" All the people of every rank and class must

8

be educated in a republic."

John Adams

In one form or another, time and time again the message comes through. If the American democracy is to continue, a system of public education must see to it that we have the citizens that will make it work.

Read the words of educators. It would be a most difficult undertaking to find a statement of the goals, the philosophy, or the responsibilities of a school, a school system, or all public education in America that doesn't include a direct reference to the development of responsible citizens. Read the time honored Seven Cardinal Principles of Education and you find among them the concern for "Civic Participation."

Read John Dewey or John Spritzberry, Robert M. Hutchins or Robert O. Kametavich, James Conant or James Hillard, Robert Sherman or Wayne Urban, Norman Deeb or Carl Kreisler who when writing about philosophy of education, history of education, foundations of education or sociology of education will all, if they deal with the obligations of education, list among the responsibilities of schools the production of "good" citizens.

Finally, if you remain unconvinced, ask a teacher--any teacher. I'll take my chances that they will most certainly tell you that one of the prime obligations of public education in America is the production of responsible citizens.

I rest my case.

Well, almost.

We human beings frequently seem to need someone or something to blame for our failures. If it turns out that we in public education are not doing such a hot job of producing responsible citizens, it would be nice to be able to blame someone or something else. Let's look around then and see who, or what, also has responsibility for this job. We can then immediately assign any failures to them.

I suppose at this point I could set up several straw men and smugly proceed to destroy them. In short order I could lay to rest imagined obligations I had created for the mass media, the churches, political figures, and special interest groups. Obviously, these are not institutions that our society has established for the purpose of perpetuating itself. I'll not make you endure the process of strawmenship.

I do what to spend some time dealing with the obligations the American family may have in the production of responsible citizens. Of course, immigration aside, the American family is the source of production of future citizens. This is not to say that producing children is an obligation of the American family. On the contrary, I know of nothing in the marriage vows that commit a couple to having children. Beyond this optional function of citizen production, I see nothing in the institution of "family" that obligates it to the perpetuation of our society. Whatever may be the function of marriage, or family without marriage, it is not an institution set up by our society for the purpose of perpetuating democracy. If it should happen that a family, or several families, should produce children who are responsible citizens, we in public education can count this as a bit of good fortune. In fact, we should be truly grateful when we find a family that is even supportive of our effort to do this job. I think it is important to emphasize what I've just said. It is not the job of the American family to produce responsible citizens. This is the job of the American public school system. If a family helps us do this job, great, but it's still our job, not theirs. In this particular instance, if we fail, to point an accusing finger at the parents neither properly fixes the blame nor excuses the lack of success. If we in public education have produced responsible citizens, it is our success, and if we haven't, it is our failure.

When a person seeks to perpetuate a society, his first concern has to be with developing means by which he can inculcate in the youth those values that are necessary for support of that particular social order. No matter what the social arrangement, it cannot be continued into the future unless the values on which it rests are perpetuated. This need to inculcate certain values in the young is as essential in American democracy as in any other social order, and this is one of the obligations of our system of public education. In some societies this would be all that the educational system would be expected to do. Because of the nature of the American democracy, more is required of the educational system that just the inculcation of supportive values. Since democracy places

10

such heavy responsiblity on the individual citizen, it
requires that he also have certain skills and knowledge. So it is that in America the educational
system has the additional responsibility of providing
the youth with the skills and knowledge that can result
in an enlightened electorate.

A RESPONSIBLE CITIZEN IS ...

To this point I've thrown the term "responsible citizen" around as though I knew what it meant. It's time now to make clear what I mean when I say "responsible citizen."

To be sure there are many possible definitions of what constitutes a responsible citizenship. To begin with, different types of societies need different kinds of citizens. A person who would be considered very responsible in one social order would possibly be a total misfit in another. In a totalitarian system the responsible citizen needs only to know what is expected of him and willingly do what he is told. Someone else is making the decisions and he need only carry them out. Obviously such a person is not a responsible citizen in a democracy. Let me repeat that, a person who simply knows what is expected of him and does what he is told is <u>not</u> a responsible citizen in a democracy.

What then is a responsible democratic citizen? There isn't complete agreement as to what constitutes a responsible citizen in a representative democracy. While I feel that the definition I'm using is certainly adequate, I'm aware that it is not the only one possible.

In a representative democracy a responsible citizen understands the system, supports the basic tenets of it, stays informed about the issues and decisions that confront his society, thinks critically about these things, and participates in the activities of citizenship.

I suppose that in any type of social order the least that could be expected of a citizen is that he understand the system. Certainly this is true in a democracy. As a bare minimum such understanding should include a grasp of the theoretical basis of democracy, the basic tenets on which the system is established, the historical development of the system, the structure

12

and mechanics, and some estimate as to the degree to which it is effectively working.

A responsible citizen supports the basic tenets of democracy. He supports the concepts of the basic worth and dignity of the individual human being and the right to self-determination, the idea of government by consent of the governed, and the principle of certain basic--inalienable if you please--human rights. He believes that representative democracy is the system of government by which these ideals can best be obtained and/or maintained. Thus he is committed to the system and process of representative democracy, and he is committed to making it work. Now, I want to make it clear here that I'm not talking about patriotism. Certainly not blind chauvenistic narrow nationalistic patriotism. So long as it isn't in conflict with the basic tenets of democracy, there is truly nothing wrong with love of country. I happen to be one who still flies the flag on appropriate occasions, gets choked up on hearing the national anthem, and can be deeply moved by the words of our founding fathers. I also happen to be one who can be moved to deep rage when confronted by an "America Love it or Leave it" bumper strip that some provincial, undemocratic jerk has put on the rear of his pickup truck. (While my commitment to the basic tenets of democracy require that I respect his right to be wrong, they do not require that I like his brand of patriotism). My point is that patriotism is fine within reason, but baseball, hot dogs, mom's apple pie, stand up for the flag, and hooray for the Bowling Green red, white and blue water tower are not to be equated with commitment to the bedrock concepts of democracy. It is this latter, not the former that is necessary for responsible citizenship.

Since representative democracy requires of the individual citizen that he be a decision maker, it should only follow that he keep himself informed regarding the matters on which he has to make decisions. Although it appears to happen, one really shouldn't make decisions on things one knows little or nothing about. If a person is going to make decisions in a responsible manner, a minimum requirement is that he be informed. All of this is just another way of saying that a responsible citizen tends to his business.

In a democracy staying informed is a necessary but not sufficient activity. A citizen is being asked to make decisions that affect not only himself but his fellow citizens and such decisions deserve better than "top of the head" or "seat of the pants" consideration. It is in this context that the need for critical thinking becomes apparent. In this regard a citizen needs not only the skills that will enable him to think critically but the mental set that will require of him that he do so.

Finally, it is not enough in a representative democracy for an individual to make decisions, even informed decisions based on critical thinking. In a democracy it is necessary that the citizen act on the decisions that he has made. This really is the crucial point. Unless the citizen is actively involved in the process, democracy hasn't occurred. Without the active participation of the citizenry in the decisions of government, all you have is the potential for democracy. A bare bones minimum of participation would at least include the obligation of voting, jury duty, and payment of a fair share of the financial support of government. Beyond this, one could possibly hope for participation in assemblies and petition for redress of grievances, the expression of opinion to elected representatives, and the active support of preferred candidates for office. The foregoing is not intended to be an exhaustive list, but it is certainly representative of the kinds of participation that would make the potential of democracy a reality.

In summary then, there are five characteristics of a responsible citizen in a representative democracy:

1. He understands the system.

2. He supports the basic ideas and concepts of democracy.

3. He stays informed about matters that confront his society.

4. He thinks critically on those matters about which he is to make decisions.

5. He participates actively in the affairs of his society.

To this point I have hoped to accomplish the following:

1. To demonstrate the connection that I feel

14

exists between human freedom and that system of government known as a democracy.

2. To explain what I'm talking about when I use the term democracy.

3. To make clear what I mean when I talk about a responsible citizen.

4. To establish the fact that in the United States of America the production of responsible citizens is the job of the public schools.

SUMMARY

Okay, I've set forth a definition of responsible citizenship and sought to establish that it's our
job in the public schools[1] to produce such people.
Let's take a look and see how well we've been doing the
job.

In the past it was possible -- even reasonable--
for public educators to excuse any failures in citizenship education by pleading lack of access. Surely if
we had only had all, or even more, of the nation's
youth, we would have successfully accomplished the job.
Since, however, the youth of America had limited access
to the public schools, it was unreasonable to hold the
schools accountable for any shortcomings in their
citizenship training. Clearly this reason will no
longer serve to excuse us, as compulsory education and
improve transportation have for quite some time given
us most of the children of most of the people. (At
least we have had them until they have reached the age
that places them beyond the clutches of compulsory
schooling). If we have failed to produce a responsible
citizenry, it isn't because we didn't have a shot at
'em.

I have made as good a case as I know how as to
why we can't shift blame for any failures in this area
to the parents.

The quality of citizenship then is, and has
been our responsibility. Let's examine the product of
our labors and glory in our successes or face up to
our failures.

---

[1]It may well be that you're wondering how I get off
talking about "we" in the public schools when I work for a
University. Good question. My response is that most of my
adult life has been spent in public education and the remainder
working with public school teachers. This is where my basic
identification lies, and I feel as though the time I have been
on the University Campus has been as a stranger in an alien land.

HE UNDERSTANDS

At the outset I want to reiterate that the job of producing responsible citizens is that of the total institution of public schools and not just the social studies teachers. I reemphasize this point because most of the material relevant to the success, or lack of success, in this area is related to social studies. In no way would I want it to be a signal that it is all right for the rest of us to get smugly comfortable and lay the sole blame on the teachers of social studies.

If there is any one thing that we in the schools are supposed to be able to do, it's to impart information. Despite anything we may say to the contrary, this is what we spend most of our time attempting to do in school. Surely such has been the case in our efforts to impart information about citizenship in the United States.

At the very outset of the school process, we teach the little children, by rote, the words to the Pledge to the Flag, the National Anthem, and other patriotic songs that are part of the heritage of Americans.[1] We teach them about Columbus, the Pilgrims, and the Minutemen. We celebrate the birthday of Washington with construction paper hatchets and the birthday of Lincoln with construction paper stove pipe

---

[1]During this time we are also working very hard at teaching the children the basic skills of communication, reading, writing, and cipering, without which any learning is most difficult. Since the founding of public education in America, this has always been a top priority item for the early years of schooling. Those who from time to time have contended that we have departed from this emphasis were perhaps confused by educational writers and have thought that what they read was an accurate reflexion of what was taking place in the classrooms. In any event, such critics didn't have the foggiest idea what they were talking about. The fact is that, whether we have succeeded or not, the development of the skills of learning have never been other than top priority in the primary grades.

hats. (Now, thanks to the U.S. Government, we aren't quite sure when to celebrate these events, but we somehow still celebrate them). We show them pictures of the cracked Liberty Bell, the Statue of Liberty, the flag, the bald eagle, and Uncle Sam.

As they progress through school we teach them about the community helpers, their local government, and state government. Often we take them to the state capital to see their government in action.[2] We show them the great documents of their nation, the Declaration of Independence, the Constitution, and the Bill of Rights. In civics we teach them about the balance of power and the responsibilities of citizenship. They hear the words of John Paul Jones and Patrick Henry, Abraham Lincoln, Thomas Jeffereson, and George Washington.

Almost without exception we have required that every child that moves through the public school have a high school course in American History. (Since this has usually been taught in the eleventh grade, we will have missed those young people who reach sixteen prior to this and drop out). In this course we teach them about the explorers and the discovery of America by Columbus and/or Erickson, the Pilgrims landing and the early colonies, the American Revolution, the westward expansion, the Civil War, the Industrial Revolution, and World War I. If we get past this we are lucky, but that's OK as everyone knows that not much has happened since then.

Beyond this we offer optional courses in various other histories, American Government, segments of American History, and some form of Problems of Democracy.

---

[2]For years I had mixed feelings about these jaunts to the capital. After spending days, perhaps weeks, telling our charges about the workings of their state government we take them to see it in action. What they see at best only vaguely resembles that which we have told them. Instead of the statesman we told them about, as likely as not they encounter buffoons and political hacks. Instead of the conscientious, enlightened deliberative body of which they read we may show them a half-present, inattentive collection of legislators. On reflection I have decided that this is perhaps one of the few times we expose the children to the realities of the workings of their government. As such, it should prove to be a good thing to do.

Even with this thumbnail sketch it should be obvious that we do not ignore our responsibility to impart information about citizenship. Such being the case, it should be reasonable to assume that the products of the public school should understand both the philosophical and historical foundations of their government as well as the structure and mechanics of the system. Beyond this, there is little evidence that we make any serious comprehensive attempt to provide the students with information regarding the degree to which the actual workings of the system fulfill the theoretical promise. Thus, it is pointless to seek evidence as to how well we are achieving this goal.

In this entire effort we have expected of the social studies teachers that they carry most of the burden. Unfair as this may be, I will turn to the social studies to begin the appraisal of the success we have met in this undertaking. Although this isn't directly related to the acquisition of information, it might be worthwhile at the outset to take a look at some studies done to ascertain the attitude of students toward social studies.[3] Perhaps there is some relationship between the way students feel about the subject area that has been the major vehicle for citizenship preparation and the amount of information they have acquired through it.

At the elementary level, according to Preston and Herman in Teaching Social Studies in the Elementary School, 1974, "...The social studies are relatively unpopular among children. ...All studies of subject preferences since 1937 known to the authors indicated that social studies ranked below most other subjects." I have checked most of the studies they listed, and it appears that they knew what they were talking about.[4] On the other hand, these studies do not indicate that social studies is often listed as the least liked subject--just somewhere there is the mediocre middle.

In 1969 Life magazine had Louis Harris and

---

[3]The "research that is done in education, sociology, and psychology isn't the most precise work that has ever existed. Some of it is notoriously sloppy. It is important to approach the acceptance of this kind of research with great caution. As a rule of thumb, the more formulas, diagrams, and arrows a study contains, the greater my skepticism about it. I mention this because I think it well to keep these studies in proper perspective.

20

Associates survey some 2500 students in one hundred
high schools to ascertain what they thought about the
courses they had taken. In this survey, history was
considered irrelevant and current affairs and politics
were considered practically useless.[5] All in all,
then, the response to social studies tended toward the
cool side of lukewarm. Perhaps we could best describe
the student attitude toward social studies as the
"blah syndrome." Such an attitude doesn't auger well
for this discipline as the vehicle for transmitting
information about responsible citizenship.

We can assume that in cases where we have
failed to effectively impart information there certainly can be no understanding. The studies that deal with
our success in imparting citizenship information are
not very encouraging. However, before we turn to these
studies let's take a look at a couple of things that
indicate that, even when we succeed in imparting the
information, understanding may not follow.

Early in the educational experience of a child
we cause him to learn the words of the Pledge to the
Flag, the National Anthem, and other patriotic songs.
In this connection, the lore of teaching is filled with
examples of the end product of this "learning" by rote
without understanding, in which students in later years
are asked to write out the words. It is in response
to such requests that students provide us with:

> "...by the dawns every night, what so loudly
> we hailed..."

> "...through the pair of us fight..."

> "...or the rams parts we watched..."

National Anthem

---

[4]Ethel E. Holmes, "School Subjects Preferred by
Children," Sixteenth Yearbook of the Nation Elementary Principal,
Washington, D.C., National Education Association, 1937, pp.
336-344.
Arthur T. Jerslid and Ruth J. Tasch, Childrens Interest and What
They Suggest for Education, N.Y., Teachers College, 1945.
Howard H. Mosher, "Subject Preferences of Girls and Boys, "School
Review, 60, January 1952, 34-38.
W. Linwood Chase and Gilbert M. Wilson, "Preference Studies in
Elementary School Social Studies," Journal of Education, 140,
April 1958, 1-5.
Joseph P. Rice, Jr., "A Comparative Study of Academic Interest

"...Thine Al the bastards cities gleam..."

America the Beautiful

"I pledge the pigeons to the flag..."

"...and to the republic for witches stands..."

"...one nation under guard..."

"...Invisible..."

"...with liberty and just sticks for all."

Pledge of Allegiance[6]

Perhaps we can assume that some time in later life they come to an understanding of the meaning and significance of the uncomprehended collection of words of their early school years. Perhaps the above examples, while attention getting, are representative of just a small minority of the children. Or, perhaps we have an adult population that still mouth these familiar words without any comprehension.

It is reasonable to assume that rare indeed is the child that goes through school without exposure to the Declaration of Independence and the Bill of Rights. The depth at which the students encounter them is another question, but kids in school are taught about these two great American documents. Despite this exposure there is reason to question whether students move from school into the adult population with any

Patterns Among Selected Groups of Exceptional and Normal Intermediate Children," California Journal of Educational Research, 14, May 1963, 131-137.
Robert L. Curry, "Subject Preferences of 1,111 Fifth-Graders," Peabody Journal of Education, 41, July 1963, 23-27.
Leon R. Capps and Linda S. Cox, "Attitude Toward Arithmetic at the Fourth and Fifth-Grade Levels," Arithmetic Teacher, 16, March 1969, 215-220.

[5]Louis Harris, "The Life Poll," Life Magazine, Vol. 66, No. 19, May 16, 1969, p.31.

[6]I am indebted for the pledge examples to Hyman Kavett who recorded them in his article, "How Do We Stand with the Pledge of Allegiance Today?" Social Education, Vol. 20, No. 3, March 1976, 136.

real understanding of the meaning of these documents. From time to time I read of a reporter or group going out into the streets of some city with a copy of the Declaration of Independence of the Bill of Rights, perhaps worded in the vernacular, to see if support can be elicited for the document. Time and time again large numbers fail to even so much as recognize the document. (Whether they would support either of these statements of American belief is the subject of a later chapter.) I have before me newspaper accounts of two such undertakings in 1975, one in Louisville and one in Washington, D.C. In one of them 47% of some 2,300 federal employees surveyed could not identify the Declaration of Independence. The account cites such responses as, "What's this? An anti-CIA thing?" and "Yes I recognize it, it's from the Communist Manifesto."[7] In the other undertaking, even though the document was identified as part of the Declaration of Independence, there were still recognition problems.[8] Now these kinds of activities can't be considered as any sort of scientific studies. On the other hand, year after year such undertakings yield depressingly similar results. It makes you wonder if we have produced people who even recognize these basic documents of our nation, let alone subscribe to their contents. In 1967, John C. Pock set out to secure the response of high school seniors to "Bill of Rights" issues as represented through eighteen specific cases. According to Pock, "several of the most fundamental tenets embodied in our heritage and expressed in the Bill of Rights," were not understood, much less supported, by many of these high school seniors.[9]

Earlier public polls taken of a national sample in 1943 and 1945 tend to bear out this contention that a substantial number of the American citizenry do not know the contents of the Bill of Rights. In

---

[7]Donald Sanders, Associated Press Writer, "Declaration of Independence - Many Polled Refused to Endorse Section of It," Park City Daily News, June 11, 1975.

[8]Chris Morris, "Truths? Maybe in 19776, But Now?" Louisville Courier-Journal, December 11, 1975.

[9]John C. Pock, Attitudes Toward Civil Liberties Among High School Seniors, Washington, D.C., U.S. Department of Health Education and Welfard, Cooperative Research Project No. 5-8167, 1967.

response to the Question, "What do you know about the Bill of Rights? Do you know anything it says?" only 23% in 1943 could list as much as one provision of the document and in 1945 this percentage had declined to twenty-one. In both cases, greater than three-fourths of those responding were unable to state one thing the Bill of Rights contained. Further, in 1954 in response to the question, "What are the first ten amendments to the Constitution called?", only 33% of a national sample replied, "The Bill of Rights."[10]

Over the last several years scholars studying the political socialization process have turned their attention to the school as one of the agents of socialization. [11] While most of these studies have concentrated on political opinions, attitudes and values, some of them have given at least passing attention to political knowledge.

In studies of school children by Roy E. Horton in 1951 and by Fred I. Greenstein in 1958, both sought in part to determine the level of political knowledge possessed by the students in their sample. In both studies it became evident that substantial numbers of youngsters were poorly informed about their government. [12]

There appears to be one benchmark study in political socialization, as it relates to the acquisition of information. This is the Langston and Jennings study of 1965 which now appears in several versions and is quoted in practically every book on

_____

[10]Hazel Gaudet Erskine, "The Polls: Textbook Knowledge," Public Opinion Quarterly, 27. (1963), 133.

[11]The term "political socialization" appears to have been coined by Herbert H. Hymen in his book Political Socialization; A Study in the Psychology of Political Behavior, N.Y. Free Press, 1959. The use made of the term varies somewhat from author to author, but the essence of it is the study of the means by which an individual acquires his political knowledge, attitudes, opinions, beliefs, and values.

[12]Roy E. Horton Jr., "American Freedom and the Values of Youth," in H.H. Remmers, Anti-Democratic Attitudes in American Schools, Northwestern University Press, 1963, p. 41.

Fred I. Greenstein, Children and Politics, New Haven, Conn., Yale University Press, 1965, pp. 57-60.

political socialization. [13] This study was designed
to determine the effect of civics curriculum on several
aspects of political socialization. Among those things
the study sought to measure was a category labeled
"political knowledge and sophistication." One of the
methods used to ascertain this, was through a series
of six questions. These questions asked the students
to identify the length of a U.S. Senator's term, the
country of Marshall Tito, the number of U.S. Supreme
Court Justices, the name of their state Governor, the
World War II nation that had concentration camps for
Jews, and the political party of F.D.R. Of the 1669
high school seniors involved in this nationwide study,
88% could name the Governor of their State, 83% knew
it was the Germans who had had the concentration camps,
64% knew F.D.R. was a Democrat, and 50% knew a U.S.
Senator's term is six years long, while only 33% appear
to have heard of the nine old men, and a mere 27% knew
of Tito the Yugoslavian partisan. Insofar as Langton
and Jennings could determine, there was a negligible
relationship between civics education and political
information. In fact, prior enrollment in courses of
the civics curriculum had little or no impact, either
positive or negative, on political knowledge. While
this conclusion seems to hold for their total sample,
it is not quite so strong for the Negro sub-group in
the study, as for them there does seem to be some
positive relationship between civics education and
political knowledge.

A study by Hess and Torney in 1965, that dealt
with the understanding of democracy of school children,
found that as much as one fourth of the pupils had
faulty concepts of democracy.[14] Studies in 1966 and
1968 by Richard Niemi and Associates, that replicated
in part the work of Hess and Torney, produced essentially the same results.[15] In both of the above studies, there was a relationship between the age of the
students and the adequacy of their understanding of
democracy in which the older students had the better
grasp of the topic.[16]

What can we make of these studies of political
socialization that touch on the effectiveness of the

---

[13]Kenneth P. Langton and M. Kent Jennings, "Formal
Environment: The School," in Kenneth P. Langton, Political Socialization, New York, Oxford University Press, 1969, pp. 84-119,
and M. Kent Jennings and Ricard G. Niemi, The Political Character
of Adolescence, Princeton University Press, 1974, p. 94.

school as an agent for promoting citizenship knowledge?
To begin with, the studies consistently support the
idea that the further a kid goes in school the more
likely he is to have increased political knowledge.
There is some reason, however, to question the role
that school plays in this increase. The Langton and
Jennings work, the only study that directed its attention to the relationship between civics education and
citizen knowledge, concluded that the school was of
little influence. At best, the question about the
amount of influence exerted by public education remains
open. Regardless of the means of acquisition, these
studies all demonstrate that a substantial number of
school students do not have even a rudimentary understanding of the basic structure of their government.
I make the preceding statement with some reservation.
The questions asked the students in the various studies
were, of course, only a very few from among thousands
that could have been asked. The decision as to which
questions were basic, crucial, and significant was
obviously subjective. Further, the most recent of the
studies cited were conducted in 1968. Beyond this, most
of the samples were drawn from specific locations that
limit the extent to which the findings can be generalized. I'm not suggesting that you discount the findings of the political socialization studies--certainly
I don't--I'm just saying that we must keep them in
proper perspective.

Beginning with a conference in 1963, supported
in its developmental stages by a grant from the
Carnegie Foundation, and initiated during the 1960-70
school year, the National Assessment of Educational
Progress came into existence. The National Assessment,
presently administered by the Educational Commission of
States, seeks to set goals (or "behavioral objectives"
--sigh) and assess progress in ten areas of educational
endeavor. One of the areas in which the National
Assessment establishes goals and attempts to measure

---

[14]Robert D. Hess and Judith V. Torney, The Development
of Political Attitudes in Children, Chicago, Aldine Publishing
Company, 1967, p. 66.

[15]Robert S. Siegel and Marilyn Brookes, "Becoming
Critical About Politics," in Richard G. Niemi, The Politics of
Future Citizens, San Francisco, Jossey-Bass Publishers, 1974,
p. 110.

[16] Ibid., p. 110.

progress is that of Citizenship. Among the seven citizenship objectives established by the NAEP is one that says that students in the schools of America should "know the main structure and functions of their governments." So it is that since 1969 this organization has had as one of its objectives the measurement of the citizenship knowledge of America's school children. Although this organization intends to assess some of its areas of concern every three years the citizenship category is scheduled for assessment only every sixth year. Thus, at this writing we only have available to us the results of the 1969-70 and the 1975-76 citizenship assessments.[17]

(The 1971-72 assessment of Social Studies did have one section which sought to measure political knowledge and attitudes.) In the initial study, 1969-70, the sample was composed of approximately ninety thousand respondents from four age groups; ages nine, thirteen, seventeen and young adults (twenty-six through thirty years old). The sampling techniques have been refined to the point that the surveyors feel comfortable in stating that their findings are representative of all Americans in the particular age groups sampled.

Since the 1969-70 assessment, both the objectives of Citizenship Education and the questions by which the assessment seeks to determine political knowledge have been refined. While this indicates a healthy attitude toward improving the assessment it unfortunately, in most cases, makes comparison between

---

[17]At this writing the following reports relevant to citizenship assessment have been distributed by the National Assessment of Educational Progress. The Education Commission of the States, 300 Lincoln Tower, 1860 Lincoln Street, Denver, Colorado, 80295:
Report No. 2, Citizenship: National Results, November 1970.
Report No. 6, 1969-70 Citizenship: Group Results for Sex, Region, and Size of Community, July 1971.
Report No. 9, Citizenship: 1969-70 Assessment: Group Results for Parental Education, Color, Size and Type of Community, May 1972.
Citizenship Objectives for 1974-75 Assessment, 1972.
Report No. 03-SS-01, Political Knowledge and Attitudes, December 1973.
Citizenship: Results Manual, December 1976.
Report No. 07-CS-01, Education for Citizenship: A Bicentennial Survey, November 1976.

the two studies an impossible task. Thus, with the exception of the few instances where comparison is possible, I'll deal separately with the two reports. (Some of the questions on each of the studes are comparable to portions of studies done at earlier times. Where it is appropriate I will mention these comparisons.)

The first assessment sought to measure citizenship knowledge in three categories: (1) "knowing basic principles of representative democratic government, (2) knowing the main structures of our government at the national, state, and local levels, and (3) monitoring the current operations of government."[18] As was the case with the political socialization studies cited earlier, the older the respondent the more likely he was to have more adequate knowledge. Thus when the seventeen-year-olds were asked to state at least one purpose for having a government, 90% could give an acceptable response and 78% knew that the president does not have the right to do anything affecting the United States that he wants. This latter item is roughly comparable to an item in the 1975-76 assessment in which 86% of those seventeen years of age felt that the president must always obey the laws of the United States. Another item on which some basis of comparison exists between the two assessments has to do with the composition of the U.S. House of Representatives. In the 1969-70 survey respondents were asked when a state might have more senators than representatives and 48% of the seventeen-year-olds picked a small population as the answer. In the second survey of 1975-76 56% in the age of seventeen category knew that the number of members of the U.S. House of Representatives that a state has varies with the population. On both of these items, to the extent that they are comparable, the seventeen-year-olds of 1975-76 did better than those of 1969-70.

Among the seventeen-year-olds in the 1969-70 assessment, 89% knew that the Senate was one of the two parts of Congress, 97% could state the name of the president, 75% the vice-president, 39% at least one senator from their state, 15% both senators from their state, 31% the congressman from their own district. Eighty-eight percent could name both major political

_____

[18]National Assessment of Educational Porgress, Report No.2, Citizenship: National Results, The Education Commission of the States, Denver, Colorado, November 1970, p.43.

28

parties and 41% could name at least one minor political party.

All in all, when you study the 1969-79 assessment things don't look too bad. Large numbers of seventeen-year-olds could give a reason for having government, knew who the President was, were aware that the President does not have the right to do as he pleases, and could name both major political parties. On the other hand, 52% of these seventeen-year-olds did not know that representation in the U.S. House of Representatives was determined by population, 61% could not name one of their U.S. Senators, 69% couldn't name their congressman, 25% could not name the Vice-President of the United States, 10% didn't know of one reason why we have government, and 3% did not even know the name of the President of their country.

Under the heading of "know the main structure and functions of their government," the 1975-76 assessment sought to determine the amount of knowledge school kids had about governmental purposes, the organization of federal and state governments, the political structure of their local government, the importance of political opposition and interest groups, the importance and means of citizen involvement, and the structure of school and student government.[19]

To this point I have refrained from making editorial comment about the quality of the national assessment program in general and the citizenship assessment in particular. I do want to comment at this time on the improvement in both objectives and questions that is reflected in the 1975-76 survey. In the main the objectives are less provincial and the questions more probing than those found in the 1969-1970 assessment.

Since once again the older students demonstrated the greater knowledge, the responses of the seventeen-year-olds will be used as the basis of this discussion.[20]

---

[19]National Assessment of Educational Progress, Citizenship Objectives for 1974-1975 Assessment, The Education Commission of the States, Denver, Colorado, 1972, pp. 19-24.

[20]National Assessment of Educational Progress, Report No. 07-CS-01, Education for Citizenship, A Bicentennial Survey. The Education Commission of the States, November 1976, pp. 21-30.

In regard to basic constitutional rights, 47% knew that one does not have to testify against himself while 97% were aware that the accused has the right to remain silent during police questioning. (Since these are both aspects of the same constitutional right, I wonder why the discrepancy. Perhaps the constant TV barrage of police reading Miranda cards explains the high recognition of one and the failure to connect it to the other.) Also under the right to due process, 99% recognized the right to counsel and the right to know of what you are being accused. Beyond this 82% knew that Congress could not establish a national church, 84% knew that the Congress could not restrict the free press, and 87% knew that the president was also restricted from doing this.

In other questions concerning the president, 91% were aware that the president could veto laws passed by Congress, and 88% knew that he could suggest legislation to the Congress. As was mentioned earlier, 86% were of the opinion that the president must obey the laws of the United States. Only 53% were aware that the president does not have the authority to appoint members of Congress.

Regarding the Constitution, 64% recognized that the U.S. is not the only country with such a document. Eighty percent knew that this is not the only country that elects its national leadership and the same percentage was aware that other countries have political parties. Seventy-two percent were aware that it is legal in this country to start a new political party. In response to the question, "Could a court in the United States decide that the United States would declare war on another country?" Seventy-nine percent responded, "No."

As was mentioned earlier, 56% were aware that the number of congressmen from a state varies with the population of that state. Forty-six percent knew that the Congress has the right to levy taxes and 22% knew that it is Congress that controls the purse strings of the U.S. Fifty-three percent knew that each state has two U.S. Senators.

As was the case with the 1969-70 assessment, we have in the results of the 1975-76 edition a mixed bag. Depending on what you look at, and how you look at it, you can either gaze on the results with complacency or view them with alarm. With the exception of the right to avoid self-incrimination, most seventeen-year-olds

answered correctly the questions about constitutional
rights and provisions. In most instances they did
equally well on questions about the duties and authority of the president. Further, most of them had an
accurate understanding as to what the courts in the
U.S. can and cannot do. Viewed from this perspective
the picture seems not at all alarming. However, if
you see fit to pick and choose in the other direction
you can find yourself--as did several newspaper
editors[21]--totally dismayed. For instance, 78% didn't
know that it is Congress that decides how the U.S. will
spend its money; 54% were unaware that it is the Congress that levies the taxes; 53% did not understand
the basic provisions of the fifth amendment; 47%
thought that the president can appoint members of Congress; and another 47% did not know that each state has
two U.S. Senators. In the light of that listing it's
easy to feel that we have good reason to fear for the
future of out country.

Lest those of us that are out of high school
decide that all of the foregoing is another sure
indication that the younger generation is going to the
dogs, let me pause here and bring reality to you "old
timers." Listen, those of you from the high school
class of 1922 and earlier: in 1954 78% of your group
didn't know that the first ten amendments to the Constitution were called the Bill of Rights. Moreover,
66% of you couldn't name your two U.S. Senators and 53%
didn't know that your state had two of 'em. Sixty-
eight percent of you old timers couldn't accurately
describe the electoral college, 85% of you could not
name the three branches of the federal government, and
87% didn't even know that all members of the U.S. house
of Representatives are elected in even-numbered years.
And as for you, high school class of 1943 through 1951,
on some of these questions you did even worse than the
old timers. In fact on the one question in the 1954
study that is comparable to the 1975-76 assessment (the
one about the number of U.S. Senators per state) only
those in the class of 1951 through 1953 did better than
the seventeen-year olds of today, while all the rest of
us "elderly citizens" did worse.[22] So much for the

---

[21]An Editor in the January 11, 1977, edition of the
Louisville Courier-Journal (which I consider a heavyweight newspaper) adopted this attitude and after "viewing with alarm," made
a lightweight plea for improved American History courses. Pity.

[22]Erskine, Op. cit., pp. 137-140.

younger generation and the dogs, and so much for smugness.

This completes the description of the various kinds of material that is relevant to ascertaining how well public education has done in producing a citizen who understands the system. What can be made of all this?

To begin with there is no comprehensive, in-depth study of the level of understanding that the American citizenry possesses regarding our system of government. In all likelihood such a study is not possible. What is available comes in bits and pieces from various kinds of studies. The bulk of these studies seek to measure information or knowledge, not understanding. Surely all of these "information" studies combined do not even begin to scratch the surface of the possible kinds of knowledge that might be examined. So it is that all of these studies together may not really measure the amount of information that is possessed by those who are moving, and have moved, through the public schools. Keeping this limitation in mind, the studies available still don't present a very encouraging picture. Substantial numbers of subjects in every study conducted, fail to demonstrate that they have command of even the most simple citizenship information. There is no reason to think that there is any understanding of the democratic system of government among this group. Whether there is understanding among those who were able to correctly respond to the questions in the various studies is a matter of sheer speculation. In truth, when seldom more than half of those surveyed know that each state has two U.S. Senators, you must wonder if there is much understanding of our system.

There is one aspect of this matter of understanding about which there is no confusion. The public schools of America do not attempt to teach their students the realities of our system of government as it is presently operating. Beyond the attempts at teaching the philosophy, history, traditions, theoretical structure, and textbook mechanics there is little effort to teach the present actual practice. For this reason, there is almost no understanding of the dissonance between theory and practice. What then does he, the citizen, understand. Not much!

HE SUPPORTS

It isn't easy to assess the extent to which Americans support the foundation tenets of their government. While it isn't terribly difficult to ascertain what someone knows or doesn't know, does or doesn't do, and even understands or doesn't understand, it is extremely hard, if not impossible, to accurately measure how someone feels. Obviously it's possible to know what someone tells you about his attitudes, beliefs, and values, and it is possible to deduce that certain behavior is possibly indicative of certain feelings, but neither of these are the same as knowing with certainty that which is inside another human being. Nonetheless, with this humbling qualification, I will do the best I can to make an assessment of support for democracy among the American people.

To try to measure the level of support, I will refer to four kinds of studies. The first of these are studies that have attempted to determine the level of support that citizens, and future citizens, have for the political institutions of our government. Second, I will give attention to alienation studies that seek to determine the degree to which Americans have withdrawn support from their government. Third, I will deal with what are known as "efficacy studies," that have undertaken to assess the extent to which our citizenry feels that it has a meaningful role to play in our government. Finally, I will look at studies that have sought to measure the degree of commitment that individuals have to the basic rights and obligations of American citizenship.

Among the many studies that seek to measure the degree to which the American citizenry support our political institutions, there is one political socialization study by Hess and Tourney that seems to be the point from which every writer starts his discussion of this topic. Who am I to be different? Their work was done in 1962 using over 12,000 school children from eight U.S. cities in grades two through eight.[1] Using a wide variety of questions aimed at ascertaining the degree of students' attachment to symbols, figures, and institutions of government, Hess and Tourney concluded:

> The young child's involvement with the political system begins with a strong positive attachment to the country; the United States is seen as ideal and as superior to other countries. This attachment to the country is stable and shows almost no change through elementary-school years.
>
> The young child perceives figures and institutions of government as powerful, competent, benign, and infalliable and trust them to offer him protection and help.[2]

Working from the same data, Easton and Dennis arrived at essentially the same conclusion and add:

> ...our data show that positive sentiment toward government, even after the child has begun to see it in impersonal terms as he moves into the later grades to elementary school, continues high.[3]

For example, they found that 84% of the eighth graders in one sample agreed with the statement, "The government usually knows what is best for the people."[4] In other such early studies involving children, essentially the same conclusion has been drawn. In 1958, for instance, Greenstein found in a national sample of children that they had very positive attitudes toward the positions of mayor, governor, and president.[5] The 1962 work of Lawson established this same kind of affirmative feeling of American children, even those in the twelfth grade, for the flag of the U.S.[6] In more recent studies the same sort of pattern has, for the most part, continued to emerge. The 1968-69 survey of youth from five countries by Farmen and German resulted in their finding that 70% of the American young people

---

[1]Robert D. Hess and Judith V. Tourney, The Development of Political Attitudes in Children, Chicago, Aldine Publishing Company, 1967, pp. 226-229.

[2]Ibid., p. 213.

[3]David Easton and Jack Dennis, Children in the Political System, Origins of Political Legitimacy, New York, McGraw-Hill, 1969, pp. 139-140.

[4]Ibid., p. 130.

scored "high" in a category they termed legitimacy of government with the remaining 30% located in the "medium" category.[7] Again, in 1970, Glenn studying four hundred twenty-two, third-through-sixth graders in southeast Michigan found that 80% reponded "yes" to the question, "Can you trust the government to do the right thing?[8]

Another means that has been employed to determine the level of support for the political institutions have been the studies that have raised questions regarding the duties of citizenship. Among the eighth-graders surveyed by Hess and Tourney there were two statements about good citizenship that received far greater support than any of several other possibilities from which the kids could choose. These were, "Interested in the way the country is run," and "Votes and gets others to vote,"[9] Both of these responses obviously expressed support for basic tenets of representative democracy. More recently 56% of the thirteen-year-olds and 68% of the seventeen-year-olds in the 1975-76 National Assessment responded in satisfactory manner to two questions that sought to determine their support for the importance of a citizen voting.[10] The piling one on the other of studies such as these has led to the general belief that the youth of America are in strong support of the symbols, figures and institutions of their government. Some of the more recent work, however, has called this idea into question. While they found that there was still a substantial reservoir of support among the young, the 1968 study by Siegel and Brooks showed some decline, partticularly among the older children. For instance, they found among the school children in the Detroit suburbs that the percent of students in the eighth grade in

[5]Fred I Greenstein, Children and Politics, New Haven, Conn., Yale University Press, 1963, p. 37.

[6]Edwin D. Lawson, "The Development of Patriotism in Children: A Second Look," Journal of Psychology, Vol. 55, 1963, 281.

[7]Russell D. Farmen and Dan B. German, "Youth, Politics, and Education," Byron G. Massialas, Political Youth, Traditional Schools, National and International Perspectives, Englewood Cliffs, N.H., 1972, p. 164.

[8]Ibid, Allen D. Glenn, "Elementary School Children's Attitudes Toward Politics," p. 55.

1966 that had responded "yes" to the Hess and Tourney question of "What goes on in government is all for the best," had been reduced from 75% to 40% in 1968 when these children were in the tenth grade.[11] Other work dealing with specific minority groups tend to further challenge the earlier assumption that there is wide-spread acceptance, among the young, of the image of our government . Even so, these contradicting surveys do not do serious damage to the conclusion that the youth of America in large numbers feel generalized abstract support for their nation. Further, at this generalized level, studies of adults seem to indicate that there is little decline in this support. Using data, parts of which went back as far as 1939, Devine concluded in 1971 that there was strong support for the procedures and symbols of the United States political system.[12] Likewise, Almond and Verba in a nationwide survey in 1960 found that 85% of their respondents listed some aspect of the American government or political tradi-tion as one of the things in this country in which they took greatest pride.[13] Further, they found that the overwhelming majority of American citizens tended to trust their government.[14] Finally, over the years the Survey Research Center has asked a cross section of the American public the very direct question. "How much of the time do you think we can trust the government in Washington to do what is right?" In 1958, 73% respond-ed "most of the time" or "always." By 1964 the percent was seventy-seven; in 1968, 61% and in 1972 it was 52%. Even after the 1973-75 period of recurring na-tional scandals there still existed a suprising amount of trust as evidenced by the 1976 figure of thirty-four percent that responded "most of the time" or "just about always." [15] Turning back to the studies of "good citizenship," we find among the adults the same general support for the ideas of participation through voting

[9]Op cit., Hess and Tourney, p. 39.

[10]National Assessment of Educational Progress, Education for Citizenship, A Bicentennial Survey, Denver, Colorado, Educa-tion Commission of the States, 1976, p. 17.

[11]Roberta S. Siegel and Marily Brookes, "Becoming Critical About Politics," Richard G. Niemi and Associates, The Politics of Future Citizens, San Francisco, Jossey-Bass Pub-lishers, 1974, p. 109.

[12]Donald J. Devine, The Political Culture of the United States, Boston, Little Brown, 1972, pp. 132-134.

and staying informed that were present in the thinking of the young. According to Almond and Verba, "In the United States 85% of the respondents talked of the ordinary man as having some commitment to his community that takes him out of involvement of purely personal affairs - even if the responsibility is minimal."[16] In connection with a study of the 1952 national election, Campbell, Gurin, and Miller developed a "citizen-duty scale" based on responses to several questions about the obligation to vote. According to their classification, 44% of their sample ranked in the highest of five "citizen duty" categories and another 40% were in the next highest group.[17] The 1976 figures from the Survey Research Center reflect this same strong support for the concept of citizen participation through voting, with the response to most voter participation questions reflecting support from between 85-90 percent of the respondents.[18] On the basis of all the foregoing I would surmise that there does in fact exist among the general population a broad, though vague, support of the institutions, symbols and figures of our government.

In contrast with the efforts to determine the extent of general support enjoyed by our government, there have been those who have sought to ascertain the extent to which there are citizens who are alienated from this government. These studies are not to

[13]Gabriel A. Almond and Sidney Verba, The Civic Culture, Political Attitudes and Democracy in Five Nations, Princeton, N.J., Princeton University Press, 1963, p. 102.

[14]Ibid., pp. 108-110.

[15]The source of this information is the Survey Research Center, Ann Arbor, University of Michigan, Election Studies:
    1958 - p. 87.
    1964 - p. 220.
    1968 - p. 289.
    1972 - p. 51.
    1976 - p. 70. The data utilized in this publication were made available in part by the Inter-University Consortium for Political and Social Research. The data for CPS 1976 American National Election Study were originally collected by the Center for Political Studies of the Institute for Social Research, the University of Michigan under a grant from a National Science Foundation. Neither the original collectors of data nor the consortium bear any responsibility for the analysis or interpretations presented here.

be confused with the various attempts that have been made to measure the degree of political cynicism that is at large in the land.

The determination of the number of Americans who are alienated from their system of government is dependent on several variables, not the least of which is the definition of the term that a particular researcher uses. Using what is apparently the most inclusive definition, Louis Harris estimates that the amount of "Disaffection and disenchantment" has increased from 29% of the American population in 1966 to 55% in 1973,[19] 59% in 1976, and 58% in 1977.[20]

David Schwartz, employing an alienation formula that he developed, made secondary analysis of Gallop poll findings and concluded that alienation had increased from 5% in 1950 to 18% in 1962.[21] Furthermore, after a review of more recent data, Schwartz, writing in 1973, concludes, "From our findings above, I believe that national studies would reveal that alienation is now also a majority position. America, I believe, has become an alienated polity." Finally, Gilmour and Lamb, in their book Political Alienation in Contemporary America, calculated that the number of Americans that are in a state of "extreme alienation" from their own government has increased from 14% in 1960 to 23% in 1972.[23] While it is impossible to draw an exact conclusion from these studies, it seems reasonable to surmise that at least as many as one-fourth of the citizenry is alienated, and regardless of the exact dimensions, the number appears to be on the

---

[16]Op. cit., Almond and Verba, p. 170.

[17]Angus Campbell, Gerald Gurin and Warren Miller, The Voter Decides, Westport, Conn., Greenwood Press, 1971, p. 196.

[18]Survey Research Center, 1976 American National Election Study, Vol. I, Center for Political Studies, Ann Arbor, Michigan, 1977, pp. 164-165.

[19]Louis Harris, quoted in "Edge of Allegiance," Robert S. Gilmour and Robert B. Lamb, Political Alienation in Contemporary America, New York, St. Martin's Press, 1975, p. 141.

[20]Taken from a radio report heard in the fall of 1978.

[21]David C. Schwartz, Political Alienation and Political Behavior, Chicago, Aldine Publishing Company, 1973, p. 236.

increase.

Obviously, not all of us are alienated. The fact that we are not estranged from our government, however, doesn't necessarily mean that we have a strong commitment to it. Certainly, if we are in strong support of representative democracy, it is necessary that we view our own participation as being a matter of importance. This then brings us to the efficacy studies. Campbell, et. al., define political efficacy as, "The feeling that political action does have, or can have, an impact upon the political process, i.e., that it is worthwhile to perform one's civic duties."[24] In other words the "efficacious citizen" believes that he has some clout, that he can make a difference, and that he does make a difference.

The studies of political efficacy center around a series of questions that have been asked over a period of years by the Survey Research Center. These questions were apparently first published by Campbell, Gurin, and Miller in 1954 in The Voter Decides.[25] The intent of these questions is to determine if the individual thinks his vote will make any difference, if he feels persons in government are concerned about what he thinks, if he feels anything he does can have an influence on government, and if he feels matters of government are beyond his comprehension. In the efficacy studies with school children the exact wording

[22]Ibid., p. 237.

[23]Robert S. Gilmour and Robert B. Lamb, Political Alienation in Contemporary America, Chicago, Aldine, 1975, p. 20.

[24]Op. cit., Angus Campbell, Gerald Gurin, and Warren E. Miller, p. 197.

[25]Ibid., pp. 187-188.

[26]David Easton and Jack Dennis, "The Child's Acquisition of Regime Norms: Political Efficacy," Jack Dennis, Socialization to Politics: A Reader, New York, John Wiley & Sons, 1973, pp. 92-95.

[27]Lee H. Ehman, Political Efficacy and the High School Social Studies Curriculum," Byron G. Massialas, Political Youth, Traditional Schools, Englewood Cliffs, N.J., Prentice-Hall, 1972, pp. 93-94.

of the Survey Research Center questions has been somewhat modified but the intent of the questions has not
been changed. Easton and Dennis, drawing on their 1962
sample of children from age 7 through 13,[26] and Ehman,
using high school students in 1967 and 1969,[27] present
information that, at best, just hints at the development of political efficacy. The problem in both of
these studies is that the researchers are dealing with
how kids think they will feel when grown, or how they
presently think adults feel, neither of which is really
a measure of their own efficacy. Let's look, then, at
the studies of adults to see if they can shed any light
on the topic. Turning again to the 1952 study reported
in The Voter Decides we find that Campbell, et.al.
ranked 27% of their sample in the highest two of five
categories of political efficacy and 34% in the two
lowest categories with the remaining 39% in the middle
group.[28] A more encouraging picture emerged in the
1960 work of Almond and Verba in which the answers to
two questions were sought to determine citizens attitudes regarding their ability to do something about
local and national regulations. They found that over
three-fourths of American citizens felt they could be
effective in influencing their government.[29] As I said
earlier, over the years the Survey Research Center
has asked a series of questions relevant to this subject. Although there are others, I'll use three that
should give you a reasonable idea of the kinds of responses they have been receiving to questions about
political efficacy. The statement, "People like me
don't have any say about what the government does,"
received 28% agreement in 1956, 29% in 1964, 40% in
1972, and 41% in 1976. In response to the statement,
"I don't think public officials care much what people
like me think," 27% agreed in 1956, 37% in 1964, 49%
in 1972, and 51% in 1976. In a slightly different
vein, but still related to efficacy, the statement,
"Sometimes politics and government seem so complicated
that a person like me can't really understand what's

---

[28]Op. cit., Campbell, et. al., p. 190.

[29]Op. cit., Almond and Verba, p. 185.

[30]Op. cit., Survey Research Center:
1956 - pp. 60-62.
1964 - pp. 96-98.
1972 - pp. 158-159.
1976 - pp. 409-410.

going on," elicited the following percentages: 1956, 64%, 1964 67%; 1972, 74%; and 1976, 72%.[30]

Obviously, the response to this last question would indicate that a frighteningly large number of American citizens feel, and have felt for some time, that the issues of government are beyond their grasp. Further, a substantial fraction of citizens over the years--perhaps as large as one-third and surely no less than one-fourth--have indicated that they feel they have little or no political clout. Beyond this, the number of those experiencing political impotence seems to be on the increase.

Okay, what do we have to this point? We have an American citizenry in which a significant number are alienated, a substantial number are disenchanted, and a goodly portion feel governmental matters are beyond their power to comprehend. At the same time we also have an American citizenry in which vast numbers apparently feel that theirs is a "good" government. Unfortunately even this general support for the "American way" seems to be on a shaky base as it appears to be grounded in vague sentimentality and lacking in depth. This brings me to this last area of study that I want to deal with in this chapter.

In a footnote I'm going to list a number of studies directly related to this aspect of support for democracy, but because they all arrive at the same conclusion, I'm not going to deal with any of them in specific detail.[31] Suffice it to say that all of these studies, from 1937 to 1976, whether they dealt with the attitudes of the young or the old, over and over again revealed a consistent pattern. First, at the

---

[31]Roy E. Horton, Jr., "American Freedom and the Values of Youth," H.H. Remers, Anti-Democratic Attitudes in American Schools, Northwestern University Press, 1963, pp. 19-60.

[32]H.H.Remmers and Richard D. Franklin, "Sweet Land of Liberty," H.H. Remers, Anti-Democratic Attitudes in American Schools, Northwestern University Press, 1963, pp. 61-72.

Herbert H. Hyman and Paul B. Sheatsley, "Trends in Public Opinion on Civil Liberties," Journal of Social Issues, 9, (1953) 6-16.

Samuel A. Stouffer, Communism, Conformity and Civil Liberties, New York, John Wiley & Sons, 1966.

abstract level Americans give strong voice to support
of the basic rights of citizens in our democracy. Second, when these abstract rights are translated into
specific situations the support for them rapidly de-
teriorates. We Americans are in favor of free speech
only so long as it is what we want to hear, favor the
protection of the rights of the minority only when we
are in the minority and support the concept of majority
rule when we are in the majority. For example, we are
all in favor of every citizen's being able to run for
office unless he happens to be a communist, or Nazi,
or.... Again and again the studies show that there is
really no depth to our commitment to the basic principles of democracy.

Most of us Americans like our country. Why
shouldn't we? We live well, even comfortably. Except
in time of all-out war, our country seldom requires of
us anything even remotely approaching a sacrifice.
Even in war, only the young are really asked to run
much risk. For most of us it's a good place to live.
From our earliest days we have been taught that this
is a good country with the "best" form of government.
So long as nothing drastic happens to upset our physical well-being and emotional balance, we enjoy a euphoric state of vague appreciation of all that our
country stands for. Apparently it is only as our ox
gets gored--as the government does something that costs
us money or blood or both--that the thin veneer of
appreciation is stripped away, and we become alienated

Herbert McClosky, "Consensus and Ideology in American
Politics." American Political Science Review, Vol, 58, No. 2,
June, 1964, pp. 361-382.

James W. Prothro and Charles M. Grigg, "Fundamental
Principles of Democracy: Bases of Agreement and Disagreement,"
Journal of Politics, 22, (1960), 276-294.

Gail L. Zellman and David O. Sears, "Childhood Origins
of Tolerance for Dissent," Journal of Social Issues, 27,
(1971), 116-126.

Richard M. Merelman, Political Socialization and Educational Climates, New York, Hold Rinehart and Winston, 1971.

Judith Gallatin and Joseph Adelson, "Legal Guarantees of
Individual Freedom: A Cross National Study of the Development of
Political Thought," Journal of Social Issues, 27, (1971),
97-101.

or disenchanted. We have little faith in our ability
to effectively deal with our government and even less
in the ability of our government to respond to our
needs. Our commitment to the basic tenets of democracy
is shallow and fleeting. We are to deomcracy the
summer soldier and the fair weather friend.

Do we support the basic tenets of democracy?
As solidly as quicksand.

National Assessment of Educational Progress, Citizenship: National Results, Denver, Colorado, Education Commission
of the States, 1970, pp. 28-36.

National Assessment of Educational Progress, Education
For Citizenship, A Bicentennial Survey, Denver, Colorado, Ed0
ucation Commission of the States, 1976, pp. 15-30.

HE STAYS INFORMED

It would be erroneous to contend that the schools have ignored the fact that a citizen needs to be informed. Too many teachers have devoted too much time to current events or the Weekly Reader or Junior Scholastic to permit the conclusion that this matter has received no attention. Why we even, from time to time, read of some school's deciding to base its entire curriculum on newspaper reading. (A practice of doubtful educational worth but of unquestionable publicity value.) In all likelihood we mention to the kids that we think highly of such TV efforts as "In the News." Certainly as we move them through our citizenship education activities, we tell them that it is an important citizenship duty to stay informed. We do all these things and more, apparently to no avail.

In his book Public Opinion and Foreign Policy,[1] James Rosenau divides what he terms the opinion-holding public into three categories: The passive mass, or mass public; the attentive public; and the opinion makers. When linked with the label "passive mass," the meaning he assigns the mass public is obvious. Likewise, the category of "opinion makers" requires no further explanation here. Rosenau includes in his "attentive public" category only those who not only stay informed about issues but also discuss them regularly. While discussion may very well be a part of the total process of paying attention, I'm willing at this point to settle for placing in the "attentive public" category one who just stays informed. In this sense, then, let's see if we can find an "attentive public."[2]

---

[1]James N. Rosenau, Public Opinion and Foreign Policy: An Operational Formulation, N.Y., Random House, 1961, p.41.

[2]James N. Rosenau, Citizenship Between Elections: An Inquiry into the Mobilizable American, N.Y., The Free Press, 1974, pp. 4-16.

Rosenau recognizes that the size of the group known as the attentive public is difficult to measure and is dependent always on the criteria used to categorize them. Nonetheless he states:

> Whatever the criteria that are used, however, the Attentive Public is rarely portrayed as a majority of the citizenry. Rather, the varying estimates usually fall well below 50 percent of the adult population.[3]

Among the lowest estimates are 10% suggested by James Rosenau[4] and 25% estimated by Donald Devine.[5]

While the typical studies done by the various opinion polling organizations are of great use in some areas, they are of little help in ascertaining how well a citizen stays informed. This appears to occur because most of the questions asked by these groups can result in an expression of opinion without revealing whether it is based on any information. On the other hand, it is possible to be well informed on an issue and still not have an opinion on the matter. Even so, it is not uncommon for the pollsters to release findings in which the "no opinions" range between ten and twenty percent. For example in February and March of 1968, in response to a Gallop Poll question about their attitudes on the Viet Nam War, 16% and 17% respectively, held no opinion even though war is a topic about which one can hold generalized opinions without benefit of any specific information.[6] Beyond this, if a pollster happens to ask a question that does require specific information about a particular issue, it is accompanied by a dramatic increase in the "I don't know" response. For example, in October of 1969, when Louis Harris Associates asked, "All in all, do you tend to favor or to oppose President Nixon's new Welfare Program?", 36% of the respondents were "not sure."

---

[3]Ibid., p. 23.

[4]Op. cit., James Rosenau, Public Opinion and Foreign Policy, p. 41.

[5]Donald J. Devine, The Attentive Public: Polyarchial Democracy, Chicago, Rand McNally and Co., 1970, p. 77.

[6]Richard M. Scammon and Ben J. Wattenberg, The Real Majority, N.Y., Coward, McCann, and Geoghegan, 1970, p. 91.

[7]Ibid, p. 75.

Likewise, when Harris asked a question in May 1968, as
to whether specific presidential candidates were in
favor of "speeding up" racial progress, 47% were "not
sure" about Ronald Reagan, 41% about Gene McCarthy, 35%
about Nelson Rockefeller, 27% about Richard Nixon, 25%
about Hubert Humphrey, and (get this) 25% were not sure
about the position of George Wallace on this question.[8]
(Of course, some of the "not sure" could perhaps be
accounted for by a lack of clarity on the part of the
candidate, but all of it can hardly be atributed to
this in the case of all candidates.) I really suspect
that if the public schools had not had some success in
conveying to future citizens the idea that they are
supposed to stay informed, all of the public opinion
polls would register higher "no opinion" responses.

In the middle nineteen sixties three studies
were conducted that sought to ascertain the extent to
which people had information relevant to foreign affairs issues. In the first of these, in 1964, John
Robinson learned that 30% of a representative sample
of the citizenry of Detroit did not know that mainland
China and Poland were communist countries[9] and 39%
didn't know that Egypt was not. Forty-two percent did
not know that England had developed and tested its own
atomic weapons, and 40% were unaware that France had
done this. In that same year Patchen learned from a
representative nationwide sample of 1429 adults that
28% didn't know that mainland China was communist; 35%
were unaware that the U.S. foreign policy had been different in the approaches taken to Russia and China; and
26% did not know that there was a war going on in Vietnam.[10] Two years later, Don Smith in another national
sampling found that only 28% of the American public had
a reasonably accurate idea of the number of American
troops in Vietnam at that time.[11] The questions and
responses listed in the foregoing are fairly

---

[8]Ibid., p. 100.

[9]John Robinson, Public Information About World Affairs,
Ann Arbor, University of Michigan, Survey Research Center, 1967,
pp.1-17.

[10]Martin Patchen, The American Publics View of U.S. Policy
Toward China, N.Y., Council on Foreign Relations, 1964.

[11]Don D. Smith, "Dark Areas of Ignorance Revisited: Current Knowledge About Asian Affairs," Social Science Quarterly,
51, December, 1970, 668-673.

representative of the level of complexity of all the questions in the three studies. At the most, these types of questions required only a minimal amount of information on contemporary issues.

Every four years since 1969, the University of Michigan's Institute for Social Research has, in connection with its national election surveys of public opinion, asked two questions that deal directly with the matter of attentive citizenry:

> Some people don't pay too much attention to election campaigns. How about you--were you very interested in this campaign, fairly interested, just slightly interested, or not interested at all in it?

> Some people seem to follow what's going on in government and public affairs most of the time whether there's an election going on or not. Others aren't that interested. Would you say you follow what's going on in government and pulbic affairs most of the time, some of the time, only now and then, or hardly at all?[12]

In response to the first question, 5% of those in the 1960 nationwide sample responded "not interested at all." And, again, 5% in 1964. In 1968 the Survey Research Center dropped the "not interested at all" response and the response for the lowest level of interest became "not much." Twenty-one percent of the 1968 sample described their level of interest as "not much"; 27% did this in 1972 and 21% in 1976.

When you combine those who responded "only now and then" with those who answered "hardly at all" in response to the second question, you get a pretty good idea of the number of those citizens who aren't even making a pretense at staying informed. In 1964, those in this uninformed group constituted 28% of the sample; in 1968, 37% and in 1972, 27%; and in 1976, 30%.

In these data, the best single measure of what I'm trying to pinpoint is the proportion of the samples that responded "all the time" or "most of the time" to

---

[12]The 1960 Election Study, Survey Research Center, Ann Arbor, University of Michigan, 1970, pp.124-125. Over the years the wording of these questions has been slightly altered but not enough to alter the sense of the question. Likewise, the response categories have been changed some making exact comparison between years impossible.

the question about their following what's going on in government and public affairs. These members of the attentive public are not great in number as evidenced by these percentages: 21% for 1960, 30% for 1964, 33% for 1968, 37% for 1972, and 38% for 1976.[13] At best slightly over a third of the American public even claim that they stay informed about public affairs.

In 1969, John Robinson had 6,834 TV watchers keep two-week diaries of their viewing habits.[14] As could be guessed, the greatest amount of viewing time was devoted to entertainment. What is startling about the findings is that 53% of those in the study did not watch so much as a single evening news program during the two weeks that they kept their diary. This study suggests, as do those that have preceded it, that at best the American public is lax when it comes to tending to its citizenship business.

Let's turn now to a survey that speaks directly to this point. From time to time you will see in the newspaper the report of a survey aimed at assessing the amount of information the citizenry has about candidates who are running for office. I have before me a clipping from the November 5, 1974, issue of the Louisville Courier-Journal that deals with such a poll. The headline reads "CBS poll finds 15% of voters know candidates." This story, from the Associated Press, appeared on the morning of the 1974 general election and told of a national survey that had been conducted one week before among 1,524 adults that were expected to vote. From this sample they were able to learn that 86% of those likely to vote could not name the congressional candidates, and 55% didn't even know that a congressional race was taking place. In the thirty-

---

[13]The material listed for each year was taken from the code book of the Survey Research Center, Ann Arbor, University of Michigan, for the corresponding year listed below.

    1960 - The 1960 Election Study, 1970, pp. 124-125.
    1964 - The 1964 Election Study, 1971, pp. 177-178.
    1968 - The 1968 American National Election Study, 1973,
           p. 20 and p. 250.
    1972 - Center for Political Studies, 1972 American
           National Election Study, I Pre-Election, 1975, 93.

           Center for Political Studies, 1972 American
           National Election Study, II Post Election, 1975,
           285.
    1976 - American National Election Study, 1976, p. 304.

four states where Senate races were in progress 66%
knew of this but only 25% could name the major senatorial candidates. In the thirty-five states where
they were to elect a governor, 56% could name the
major candidates, 19% could name one and 13% could name
none. What this all says is that one week before the
election among those likely to vote, 86% did not know
who was running for congressman; 75% could not name the
senatorial candidates in their state; and 44% did not
know the names of those candidates who were running
for governor. There, friend, is your informed citizenry in the raw. In this survey there was no room
for the respondents to wiggle out with some expression
of opinion; either they knew or they didn't. They
didn't.

In Political Participation, Lester Milbrath estimates that 33% of the American citizenry are literal-
ly unaware of the political world and another 60% are
just spectators.[15]

I suppose that it was information such as the
foregoing that prompted Alfred Hero to write:

> ...the majority of Americans have paid relatively little
> or no attention to most international and national issues
> ...accurately informed persons are few--about 5% of the
> population... On most of the questions discussed here,
> however, a third to as much as two-thirds of the samples
> may be typed as ignorant, apathetic, or both.[16]

Before leaving this topic, I want to give a
little attention to the performance of teachers--those
who work in the institution set up to produce responsible citizens--on the matter of staying informed. From
time to time the Research Division of the National Education Association produces a report that says that
the average teacher reads one or two newspapers a
day.[17] Not only that, most of them read the local and
national news stories daily. Or so we tell the NEA,
who in turn tells the world. We also all own TV sets

---

[14]John P. Robinson, "The Audience for National TV News
Program," Public Opinion Quarterly, 35, Fall, 1971, 404-405.

[15]Lester W. Milbrath, Political Participation: How and
Why Do People Get Involved in Politics? Chicago, Rand McNally,
1965, p. 21.

and watch the evening news. It would seem that we
would be much better informed than your average citizen. Such being the case, why is it that my experience, limited though it may be, will not support this
conclusion? During my eighteen years in public education in the state of Florida, it was my experience
that most teachers were not well informed about international, national, state or local issues,or even those
political issues that affected them in a very direct
way. Since coming to Kentucky, I have from time to
time asked graduate students (almost all teachers) in
my classes about particular social issues. The response has tended to support my earlier conclusion. In
particular I recall one week in which I asked three
different classes about two current national events.
(The total number involved was around one hundred graduate students, most of whom were public school teachers.) I asked them what they knew about--and how they
felt about--President Nixon's impounding funds appro-
priated by the Congress for improved water treatment,
and what they knew about and felt about Judge John
Sirica's sentencing some men for breaking into an
office in the Watergate building in Washington, D.C.
Both of these events, it seemed to me, were of crucial
importance to our nation. In the first instance, the
President was in the process of changing the traditional (and, as was later established, legal) relationship
between the executive and legislative branches of our
government. In the second instance, even a casual ob-
servation of the events leading to this sentencing
would have led one to the conclusion that something
was very much amiss in this "Watergate" business. In
one class section, not one person knew of either of
these events; in no section did as much as a fourth of
the class know of both events and more than one-half
in each class did not know of either event.

I'm well aware that that which I've just related
is in no sense a scientific study. It isn't even necessarily representative of the students I've taught,
let alone the graduate students of this University or

---

[16]Alfred Hero, "Public Reaction to Government Policy,"
John P. Robinson, Jerrold G. Rusk, and Kendra B. Head, Measures
of Political Attitudes, Ann Arbor, University of Michigan,
Survey Research Center, 1968, p. 24.

[17]For example, Research Division, National Education
Association, Reading and Recreational Interests of Classroom
Teachers. Washington, D.C., NEA, 1967, pp. 7-13.

the teachers of Kentucky, or the teachers of Florida, or the teachers of the U.S. But, every time I've done this kind of completely unscientific sampling the results have been essentially the same. While this clearly doesn't establish the contention that the teachers of the U.S. are not well informed about social issues, it surely doesn't do anything to support the idea that they are.

How well then is your American citizen informed about the issues that confront him? Abysmally!

HE THINKS CRITICALLY

Look at the written philosophy of any school
(if they have one and can find it), and you will find
contained therein a statement that they seek to develop
critical thinkers. Read the written objectives of
any social studies course, or math course, or English
course, or science course, or practically any other
course, and more likely than not you will find a goal
that centers on the development of the skills of
critical thinking. If there is any one thing we are
for in the public schools, it is "critical thinking."
This must be so, because over and over again we say
it's so.

To assess our success in this area, I'm not
going to turn to the scholars but rather to the politicians and the public relations folk who work for
them.

During the many years that my Congressman has
been in the House of Representatives he has never
missed a roll call. This is an enviable record that is
without parallel in the history of the U.S. When he
runs for office, he does so without seeking or
accepting financial contributions. Such a practice,
when possible, must reduce the possibility of influence by special interest groups. To the extent that I
know him, I like my Congressman. While I don't subscribe to some of his political beliefs, I think of him
as a conscientious, intelligent, and honorable man.
From time to time when he is home, he speaks to the
local Kiwanis Club of which we both are members. The
sum and substance of his speech each time is, "Fellows,
we have a lot of problems facing the Congress and country. Their solution will require careful thought and
hard work. This is a great country and we will solve
our problems." He does not talk about specific issues
and how he stands on them. Why should he? We don't insist that he do so. Neither does anyone else. For
whatevere reason we elect him over and over again, it is
not because we have made a critical analysis of how he
stands on crucial issues. Shoot, we don't even know.

52

We are fortunate. At least he is conscientious, intelligent, and honorable. Many other American citizens
are not so lucky.

If you want to understand the degree of critical
thinking done by the American citizenry, you must examine the level at which they are approached by those
who want something from them. Are the American people
approached as though they practice critical thinking?
Do those who want something from the American people
provide them with data that can be understood, docu-
mented, analyzed, categorized, and evaluated? Let's
take a look.

Political candidates want something from the
American electorate. One of the ways they try to get
what they want from the citizenry is through political
advertising. Political advertising, then, should yield
for us the information we need to determine the degree
to which the citizenry thinks critically.

In the 1972 presidential election campaign even
the most casual observer could safely guess that in
Alabama Richard Nixon was going to beat the stuffing
out of George McGovern. By the same token, it was reasonable to assume that the Alabamians would vote to
return the very popular John Sparkman to the U.S.
Senate. Further, because of the heavy Democratic re-
gistration, it was likely that most candidates of that
party would win state and local elections unless the
Republicans could ride in on the coattails of Nixon.
In an effort to achieve this coattail effect a series
of ads was run in the Huntsville, Alabama, paper. (Such
ads may have been placed in other Alabama newspapers
for all I know. I just happen to have seen those from
Huntsville.) The headline of one reads "Be careful
Alabamians." The ad advises the Alabamians to make sure
that their vote counts and that they don't vote for
McGovern through error. It points out that the ballot
is long and confusing and that the name of President
Nixon isn't even on it. However, this will present no
problem if the voter will just follow the instructions
given in the ad. Simply pull the one big lever by the
picture of the elephant or, if voting by paper ballot,
make one X in the big circle at the top of the ballot
under the picture of the elephant. This method of
voting, the ad assures the reader, is the easy and sure
way to "send McGovern your message by voting for the
Nixon ticket." The ad goes on to say that if you vote
in any other fashion you may help elect McGovern and
urges that you don't take any chances and pull the

big lever or mark the circle. This ad had pictures
with arrows drawn, of course, to show the voter exactly
what to do. Obviously the intent of the ad was to capitalize on the anticipated Nixon vote and try to ride
the rest of the ticket into office through conning
people into voting for the entire Republican slate via
the "big" lever or circle. Beyond this, one of the
things about this ad that intrigued me is the assumed
need to instruct some of the voters to look for pic-
ures. Apparently it was thought that the voters were
not only stupid but illiterate as well. I wonder who
they thought would be able to read the ad to these
unfortunates. Surely, you say, the Alabamians were
able to see through this ploy. Perhaps, I reply, but
the Democrats weren't too confident that such was the
case. In response to this advertising campaign the
Democrats countered with an advertisement that told
Democrats how they could split their vote if they so
desired. The first instruction was "Don't Pull the Big
Lever." The ad then went on to tell the voters how to
pull the small John Sparkman lever. Regarding the
presidential election, it advised that one could pull
either the small "electors levers" under the elephant
or the rooster, depending on whether one wanted to vote
for Nixon or McGovern. In this election the Alabamians voted overwhelmingly for Nixon (who besides Massachusetts, Washington, D.C., and me didn't?) and for
John Sparkman. Perhaps this would have occurred with
or without all of these advertising campaigns, but this
is beside the point. The point is that this is the
level at which the politicians approach the electorate
in and around Huntsville, Alabama.

Rare indeed is the politician who approaches us
as though we even have good sense. Far and away the
majority of the material that is aimed at the American
electorate in the campaign seasons is some form of propaganda aimed at producing the desired emotional reaction for this or that candidate. Yet, if this approach
didn't work, if it failed to produce the desired response, its use would have ceased long ago. Every
political season produces a seemingly endless parade of
the use of the various techniques of propaganda.

Who among us hasn't witnessed the endless
barrage of political name calling? Name calling that
ranges from the gross, with such epithets as "nigger
lover," "leftist," "fascist," "pinko," and "rightest,"
to the sophisticated "militant marxist" and "arch-con-
servative." Perhaps you have heard with amusement the
tales of the 1950 Florida U.S. Senate primary between

Claude Pepper and George Smathers. Through the back-
woods of North Florida the word was spread by Smathers
supporters that Pepper had been caught "matriculating"
at the University of Florida. Not only that, it was a
known fact that his brother was a "homo sapiens" and
his sister a "thespian." Smathers won the primary,
which at that time in that state was tantamount to
election. Really not such a laughing matter.

When it comes to the use of the glittering generality technique of the propagandists, the political
arena is without peer. All of us, and the politicians
who appeal to us, are for law and order, quality education, the Constitution, God, mom's apple pie, hot
dogs, baseball,...... And during the campaigns we get
these glittering generalities in full measure. Likewise, we are exposed to a continuous effort to get us
to transfer the high regard we hold for the traditional
symbols of our country to first one candidate and then
another. Imagine if you will the ideal "transfer"
candidate with his George Washington wig and Abraham
Lincoln beard, standing in front of the Jefferson Memo-
rial with his Bible in hand, the red and white cover of
which has been embossed with a blue Statue of Liberty.
Give your heart a little tug? So would my favorite
transfer type ad which was run by a Kentucky gubernator-
ial candidate in 1975 with a picture of himself on the
outside balcony of the Capitol Building with an American flag on his right hand and a flag of the Common-
wealth on the other. The text of his ad, of course,
called for a return to the Constitution and contained
a Bible verse. Beautiful! Even so he didn't win.

No political campaign would be complete without
that old propaganda faithful, the testimonial. For as
far back as memory permits, I can see the faces of the
famous from the entertainment, or sports, or literary
or religious world beaming as they extend the hand of
blessing over one or another party or candidate in the
political parade. No doubt you will remember those two
experts in governmental matters foreign and domestic,
Joe Garagiola and Pearl Bailey, urging us to support
Gerald Ford in the 1976 presidential election. No
doubt you can also remember several hundred other examples of the political use of the testimonial. Let
me add a heart-warmer to your collection. It consists
of an ad placed in a local paper in 1975 by the mother
and father of a candidate for the city commission in
which they urge that you vote for their son. Now,
friends, that's a testimonial. He didn't win either.

Then there is the "plain folks" propaganda approach to political campaigning. You know, it's the
picture of the candidate seated in the living room with
his loving family surrounding him. Or the candidate in
the hard hat (and necktie) talking with the laboring
man. Or the candidate in shirtsleeves playing checkers
with one of the old-timers around the courthouse
square. Or better still, the candidate with coat slung
over shoulder strolling through the farm rows, pre-
sumably the land of his birth, discussing crops. Yes
sir, here he is a man of the people, just one of us.
During the presidential campaigns of 1976 George
Wallace, the self-appointed spokesman for the hard-
working, tax-paying, God-fearing middle American, held
this plain folks ground until "born-again" jeans-wear-
ing Jimmy Carter strolled in from the peanut farm and
took it away from him. My favorite "plain folks" candidate for all time is the late Sidney J. Catts who ran
for governor of Florida with the slogan, "the poor
man has only three friends: Jesus Christ, Sears Roe-
buck, and Sidney J. Catts." He won.

The best recent example of the political use
of the cardstacking form of propaganda can be found in
recalling the Carter-Ford debates. On those rare occasions when the representatives of the news media
could get the candidates to actually respond to a question that had been asked, they would invariably give a
stacked-deck answer. Carter would tick off facts and
figures--all of them accurate--that would clearly demonstrate that we were on the brink of economic dis-
aster. In response Ford would cite information chapter and verse--all of it accurate--that demonstrated
with certainty that we were well on the way to economic recovery. Neither was lying. Neither of them
was letting it all hang out. Both were dealing from a
stacked deck. Some debate.

Finally, a few words about the political use of
the propaganda technique known as "the bandwagon." The
idea here, of course, is to convince everyone that
everyone is going to vote for a particular candidate,
in hopes that everyone will decide to get on the bandwagon. If a poll can be secured that shows that a
candidate has a majority of the prospective voter support, it is to his advantage to have this become public
knowledge. If a legitimate poll cannot be found, it is
not unheard of to create such a poll for imagination
of some less than reputable polling organization and
leak the "confidential results of overwhelming support

to some member of the press. You know, "a source close
to the candidate revealed that a secret statewide
survey conducted by Klutz, In., found Spritzberry
leading Saffaticker by a wide margin in the race for
dog catcher." So sensitized are the political aspir-
ants to the need for the bandwagon effect that they go
to great lengths to muster demonstrations of strong
support. This, in major campaigns, is the job of one
who is known as the advance man. It is his job to see
to it that there are large crowds at the airport, the
train station, the "spontaneous" rally, and the audi-
torium. Hear the words of an advance man:

> It's always more impressive to fill a small hall than it
> is to half fill a huge hall. It looks more impressive,
> it feels more exciting, to walk into a five-thousand
> seated hall that's packed to the rafters than it is to
> see thirty-thousand people in Yankee Stadium.[1]

In the early days of television coverage of the
national political conventions, the attempt to create
the bandwagon effect was carried to comic extremes. On
the day of the presidential nominations (or "THE MAN
WHO" day as it is commonly called), great effort was
made to create the impression that each nominee had
overwhelming support, through attempting to pack the
galleries and through the huge demonstrations. You
remember the scene: "I give you the man who will be the
next President of the United States, Sam Spritzberry!"
Into the aisles flow a mob who just happen to have
Spritzberry signs, hats, banners, placards, and buttons.
Miraculously, some of the delegates have thought to
bring their musical instruments, and wonder of wonders,
they all seem to know the same tunes. Around the
aisles of the convention hall they lead the demonstrators to the sound of "Hot Time in the Old Town Tonight."
Everyone is for Spritzberry! Ten, twenty, thirty,
forty-five minutes the demonstration goes on as the
Chairman pounds the gavel and pleads, "The delegates
will please clear the aisle." Finally the demonstration subsides and the seconding speeches begin. Having
finished with Spritzberry, we hear, "I give you the man
who will be the next President of the United States,
Utie Saffaticker!" Into the aisles flow a mob who just
happen to have Saffaticker signs, hats, banners, placards and buttons. Miraculously, some of these cele-
gates also have thought to bring their musical

---

[1]Jerry Bruno and Jeff Greenfield, The Advance Man, N.Y.,
William Morrow, 1971, p. 58.

instruments, and wonder of wonders, they all seem to know the tunes. Around the aisles of the convention hall they lead the demonstrators to the tune of "Happy Days Are Here Again." And on and on, ad absurdum. What we in the TV audience did not witness was the scene in the convention hall lobbies during the seconding speeches for Spritzberry as the paid demonstrator removed his hats, and buttons, laid down his signs and placards, and picked up and put on those of Saffaticker. Let's hear it for the bandwagon!

The appeal to the American voter is not to the intellect but to the emotion; we are given propaganda, not information; images, not people; platitudes, not issues. Says professional political "tub thumper" Hal Evry of the Public Relations Center in Los Angeles:

> What we look for in a candidate is lots of money, an I.Q. of 120 and his promise to keep his mouth shut. The only reason we asked for the 120 I.Q. is so he's smart enough to understand the reasons for keeping his mouth shut. While the campaign is going on, we have him take a long vacation or go down to South America... No speeches, no debates. He faces the people only on TV, in the newspapers and by direct mail.[2]

Think back to the 1960 Kennedy-Nixon debates. Everyone concedes that Nixon lost and Kennedy won. Won what? Who today, or the day after a debate, could spell out for you where either Kennedy or Nixon stood on any issue? Precious few, if any, of us could even give an accurate account of what they said. Yet, Kennedy won the debate. No, what Kennedy won was the Emmy--he looked better, came across better, and put on a better performance. Kennedy won the image contest and Nixon didn't, a lesson that was not lost on Nixon the next time around. In this same vein I recall one governor's race in Florida in which I was actively supporting the candidacy of an individual who wasn't going to win any "mister handsome" contest. On several occasions individuals told me that they just couldn't vote for him because he was so ugly. Thank God we didn't have television in Abraham Lincoln's day. Political candidates win and lose elections on the image--not the portrait of their character--the image that they manage to

---

[2]David Chagall, "How People Vote - An Eye-opening Look at How Experts See It and Shape It." Family Weekly, October 19, 1975.

project.

Ray Price, A Nixon speech writer, said it in
1967:

> We have to be very clear on this point: that the response
> is to the image, not to the man, since 99 percent of
> the voters have no contact with the man. It's not what's
> there that counts, it's what's projected--and carrying
> it one step further, it's not what he projects but rather
> what the voter receives. It's not the man we have to
> change, but rather the received impression.[3]

Not so, say Richard Scammon and Ben Wattenberg.
The typical American voter makes his decision on the
basis of issues. According to these authors the typical American has been voting in recent years in terms
of what they describe as the "Social Issue." Through
his vote, Scammon and Wattenberg believe the voter has
been saying:

> I am a moderate man, but I must tell you that I have
> been unnerved in recent years. I am upset by crime;
> I am distressed about drugs; I am against disruptions
> and riots; I disapprove of the change in morality;
> I am against forced busing for my children into slum
> neighborhoods; I am concerned, with mixed feelings,
> about the racial situation.[4]

According to them, it is concern for these
kinds of things that they describe as the social
issue that permeates the thinking of the typical
American voter as he enters the polling booth. Suppose
that what these two gentlemen contend is accurate. How
do the political candidates deal with us as they discuss solutions to these problems that "unnerve" us?
They deal with us as though we don't have good sense.
Of course they are for "law-and-order" and they, when
elected, will solve this highly complex, complicated,
most difficult problem of increased crime by "not
coddling the criminal." Or, "By God, we'll restore the
death penalty and that will solve the crime problem."
We can get rid of the drug problem by cutting off the

---

[3]Joe McGinniss, The Selling of the President, 1968,
"Memorandum; Ray Price, November 28, 1967;" New York, Trident
Press, 1969, p. 204.

[4]Richard M. Scammon and Ben J. Wattenberg, The Real
Majority, N.Y., Coward, McCann and Geoghegan, 1970, p. 275.

supply or imposing stiffer penalities on the pusher and/or users. We can stop the riots and disruptions by throwing the punks in the slammer. We can restore the "old" morality by stopping abortions, outlawing poronography, catching the welfare cheats, curbing the unions, and most important, getting God back into the public school classroom. We sure as the devil will stop this "forced bussing." After all, the racial problem would have been solved by now if those damn niggers and other outside agitators would leave things alone. Or, if these solutions don't suit you, we can soak the rich, stamp out poverty, legalize crime, protect the environment, and return to nature. <u>Simplistic answers to complex problems</u>. Politicians pandering to our worst emotions and fears, substituting slogans for answers, appealing to our emotions, giving us demogogic harangues instead of reasoned discourse.

So it is that whether we are voting on images or issues, the approach is the same. Instead of hearing what we need to know, we get what we want to hear.

Chief among those things we want politicians to tell us is that you get something for nothing. Legion is the number of successful political candidates who have promised us a succession of governmental services at no additional cost. Why, I recall that in 1966 we elected a man governor of Florida who promised to make us number one in education (something that would have required gargantuan financial outlay) without levying any new taxes. He turned out to be unable to deliver on either count, but he did get elected. Sometimes this something for nothing pitch is cloaked in more reasonable terms but it boils down to the same thing. You know, "I am a businessman. You know how much waste there is in government. Send me to the Capitol and I will institute sound business practices that will save tremendous amounts of money which we can use to finance all the needed services that I have promised you without an increase in taxes." Sounds great. It hasn't happened yet.

And so we elect them, not really knowing who they are or where they stand. In 1970 when Bill Brock was running for U.S. Senator from Tennessee he posted billboards over the state that said, "Bill Brock Believes." This was too much, even for the typical voter, so in response to criticism, he added more to the sign so it read "Bill Brock Believes What You Believe." He was elected United States Senator from Tennessee.

Once in office the successful candidate continues to function as though we will view his conduct with something less than a critical eye. And he is safe in making such an assumption. Unless his misconduct in office is so very blatant as to make it impossible to ignore, we will sit still with little or no explanation for gross misfeasance and malfeasance. Witness the unchallenged illegitimate junkets, political use of the franking privileges, conflict of interest, misappropriation of funds, kickbacks, and corruption that are daily reported but not remedied. Witness the traditional public relations tactics with which each fresh scandal is met: the denial, the dismissal as irrelevant, the partial admission, the attempts to discredit and harass the complaining party, the trumped up exoneration, and the phoney investigation. Witness a succession of national leaders who, on the claim that issues are too complicated for the American people to understand, and in the name of national security, have with ever-increasing frequency misinformed and deliberately misled our citizenry. This to the point that David Wise writes, "By 1972 politics of lying had changed the politics of America. In place of trust, there was widespread mistrust; in place of confidence, there was disbelief and doubt in the system and its leaders."[5] Enough. There is no need for me to labor this further with more examples from the inexhaustible supply of evidence.

Yes, the schools state again and again that they intend to produce a citizen who thinks critically. The only success we appear to have had is that we seem to have produced a citizen who is vaguely aware that he ought to reach his decisions on a rational basis. This success perhaps accounts for our tendency, after we have made our customary emotion-based decision, to feel the need to construct a rational basis of support for it. Be this as it may, the evidence is overwhelming that we have produced a citizen who has neither the skill nor the inclination to think critically. He thinks critically? In a pig's eye.

---

[5]David Wise, The Politics of Lying; Government Deception, Secrecy, and Power, New York, Random House, 1973, p. 26.

HE PARTICIPATES

This is not going to be a long chapter. Why beat a dead horse?

In the public schools we try to have our students participate in a wide range of citizenship activities. In an effort to give them experience in participatory self-government we have them elect officers of various descriptions to assorted classes, clubs, councils, and governments. In this connection our schools periodically blossom forth with the full trappings of political campaigns. We establish student councils or governments, at times even in the elementary schools, so the students may "participate" in the governance of the institution. We bring in voting machines and have them participate in mock elections. In many locations we have them take over city government for a day, and in some we have them serve on advisory bodies for both governmental and civic organizations. We send them to Girls State and Boys State. Lord knows, we involve the students in enough campaigns for worthy causes. We often involve them in community improvement projects. On occasion the students even instigate such projects and work to secure community support for them. All to no avail.

The average United States citizen isn't very big on participation. On election day, if he thinks about it at all, he may or may not darken the door of the polling place. In fact, he may not have taken the trouble to register and couldn't vote should the spirit so move him. Chances are he hasn't discussed the election with anyone. He most certainly hasn't attended a political meeting, worked for a candidate or political party, put a candidates bumper sticker on his car, or worn a campaign button. You can bet your life that he hasn't invested any of his hard earned money on the political campaign of any candidate. He doesn't write letters to public officials and he doesn't write newspaper editors about political matters (or anything else as far as that goes). He won't sign petitions, participate in protest meetings and marches, or get involved in any civil disobedience or demonstrations. (In fact he doesn't even approve of the latter activities.) Your average citizen is really very much inclined to stay the hell out of things political and governmental. Unless it is his ox that is being gored he is willing to ignore his government--in fact he would rather. He will serve on a jury if he can't find some way to get excused, he will pay those taxes that he can't evade without imminent risk of jail, and he will obey those laws that are covenient and break those that are inconvenient when there is little chance of getting caught.

Look at a _few_ facts and figures:

*In the 1976 national election, of the 146 million Americans who were eligible to vote, only 68% were registered. Of those eligible to vote, eighty-three million, 57% went to the polls and cast a ballot. In the national election of 1972, 56% of those eligible voted. In 1968 it was 61% and in 1964 the percent was 62.

*In the May, 1976 primary election in Warren County, Kentucky, of the 23,505 registered voters, 27% managed to make it to the election booth. Sometimes as many as 48% of the registered voters of Warren County will cast a ballot, but seldom--very seldom--will the vote exceed this figure. On a recent election day, May 23, 1978, only 8% of the Warren County voters participated. However, the 1976 percent is more nearly representative of "normal." (Now, neighbor, before you throw any rocks at Warren County, Kentucky, run down to the Court House and check the turnout for your own county over a period of time.)

*In 1976, 69% of the American people did not talk to anyone about the presidential political campaign.[1]

*In the 1976 national election, 8% of the American people had worn a candidates button or put his bumper strip on his car, 9% had given money to a political candidate, 6% had attended a political meeting, and 4% had worked for one of the political candidates.[2]

---

[1] Survey Research Center, 1977, p. 261.

[2] _Ibid._, pp. 262-263.

*As of 1976, seventy-two percent of the American citizenry had <u>never</u> written a letter to a public official.[3]

The American citizen participates? Not much.

---

[3]<u>Ibid</u>, p. 264.

SUMMARY

In this section I have taken a look at how well we in public education have accomplished the task of producing responsible citizens. The picture that has developed is rather bleak. I suspect that most of us knew that it would be, even before I began. Even so, now we have some documentation for that which we probably knew all along.

In all of the material I have amassed, it has been necessary to deal in generalities. In every case there are exceptions. We do have responsible citizens in these United States of America. There are those among us who understand the system and support it, stay informed, think critically, and participate in its function. Unfortunately their number is not large.

Of course there are individual cases that in no way represent the picture of the average citizen that has emerged. Further, there are subgroups--minority groups of varying description--that more recent socialization studies have demonstrated do not fit the general pattern. In the same fashion, studies over the years have shown that the forlorn prototype of citizenship that has surfaced from the mass of information I have presented is not equally distributed throughout the population. In this regard it is paradoxical that, while studies seem to show that the educational system has little effect on the development of responsible citizens, the more education the individual has the likelier it is that he will function as a responsible citizen.

Having noted the exceptions, I'll now describe the typical citizen of the United States of America. He has some vague understanding of the outlines of the governmental structure within which he lives, but little real grasp of how it is supposed to work and even less for how it is really working--or failing to work. He has a generalized positive feeling about his country and at a remote, abstract level is supportive of the basic tenets of democracy with which he happens to be familiar. However, when these basic tenents are put to specific and concrete test, his support rapidly fades. He doesn't tend to his business as a citizen and has to be pounded over the head with an issue before he even beomes aware of it. Once he is aware of a decision that confronts him, his response will most likely be at an emotional level or in terms of a set of stereotypes and seldom if ever as a result of critical thinking. He doesn't feel that he makes any difference in the affairs of his government and, except when some governmental act really inconveniences him, prefers to remain apart from the whole operation. There is no way in which he can be labeled a responsible citizen. Au contraire, compared to the model citizen, he is a civic slob.

There are many agencies that studies show have some influence on the development of a citizen. Chief among these socializing agents are the family, peer group, and mass news media. There is also the institution known as public education. If these other agencies help develop a responsible citizen, great. If they serve to deter the development of such a citizenry, too bad. Whether these agencies help or hurt does not in any way alter the fact that the production of responsible citizens is the job of public education-- these other agencies can just make our job either harder or easier; they cannot absolve us of this obligation that is ours. We have failed.

PART III

WHAT'S WRONG?

IS IS POSSIBLE?

Throughout this book I've been talking about the model--the ideal--this "responsible" citizen as though I thought it reasonable to expect people to become such an individual. Is this goal of a responsible citizen really possible, or is this just some unattainable concept that is used to shame the American people, condemn the public school teachers, and provide the few who approach such an ideal with a smug feeling of condescension? Taken in a literal sense, the obvious answer to the question is yes. Of course it's possible because we have amongst us those who substantially fulfill the criteria of responsible citizenship. Perhaps you are such a person. Lord knows I work at it. But, that really begs the question because it isn't really whether we can produce some or a few; the question is, can we reasonably expect to produce a substantial portion of the American public who will fulfill their citizenship responsibilities? Just as it is ridiculous to expect that every person in the U.S.A. will measure up to the criteria, it is equally frivolous to point to a few, and say this answers the question. However, the existence of this few does mean that such a citizen can exist.

Even if it is possible, it is really desirable to make a serious attempt to develop an active and enlightened citizenry? After all we've survived and flourished over two hundred years without it and, all in all, things have gone pretty well. Isn't it really better if we just keep talking participatory citizenship, while in fact a small number of attentive citizens keep an eye on the active few who actually run things? Hasn't this worked pretty well for us? Wouldn't the masses, if they got with the program, just mess things up? Perhaps.

Some of the studies mentioned in an earlier chapter showed that those who are in positions of leadership have a much stronger commitment to the basic tenets of democracy[1] than does the general populace. For example, those who presently appear to be in the

68

leadership positions in our society express much stronger support for freedom of speech and the rights of the minority, even in specific concrete situations, than does the public at large. Because of this, there are those who contend that democracy is in much safer hands than it would be if more of the citizenry became involved in the political process. If, as is sometimes speculated, it is true that the American people would vote against the Bill of Rights if given the opportunity, it would not be a good thing for the masses to get much involved in the business of government. Far better to keep the natives passive and euphoric, while the activists who are really committed to basic human rights run the show. Let the common herd, in their infinite wisdom--or more likely ignorance--choose their leaders and go back to sleep. Perhaps, in sum and substance this is what Weissberg is talking about as he describes the electoral competetion form of democracy.[2] Certainly this is the position of those who subscribe the the "elitist theory" of democracy.[3] Those who hold with this elitist theory honestly feel that if the masses become actively involved they will foul things up beyond all recognition. Why not leave well enough alone?

At this point I'm going to do exactly what you would expect and cite reasons why I don't think we should settle for an elitist approach to deomcracy. To begin with, things haven't really gone all that well. Even with their supposedly greater support of the basic democratic principles, the leaders haven't done such a red hot job of protecting the individual rights of American citizens. In fact it is easy to assemble a long list of instances over the years in which just the opposite has occurred. Even the most well-intended political leaders haven't produced a faultless record.

---

[1]The leading one of these is the work by McClosky: Herbert McClosky, "Consensus the Ideology in American Politics," American Political Science Review, Vol. 58, No. 2, June 1964, pp. 361-382.

[2]Robert Weissberg, Political Learning, Political Choice and Democratic Citizenship, Englewood Cliffs, N.H., Prentice-Hall, 1974, pp. 176-177.

[3]A good description of the elitist theory can be found in: Thomas R. Dye and L. Harmon Ziegler, The Irony of Democracy; An Uncommon Introduction to American Politics, Belmont, California, Wadsworth Publishing, 1971, pp. 127-147.

Suppose for a moment that some really unscrupulous
political leaders were to get into positions of real
power and decide that they wanted to stay there. (A
possibility that isn't beyond comprehension.) Suppose
that these persons gained access to the office of President of the United States. Imagine, if you will,
that these people were really skilled in the techniques
of propaganda, the manipulation of the mass media and
other such skills from the P.R. man's bag of tricks.
Suppose these people then set out to discredit, intimi-
date, and violate the constitutional rights of any who
opposed them, even to the point of preparing a list of
enemies who were to be "screwed." Imagine that they
launched a deliberate and concerted campaign to discredit and emasculate the news media. Suppose they set
out to gain control over the judicial system. Suppose
in the name of national interest and national emergency
they set out to further weaken and discredit an already
weakened and discredited Congress. (If this listing
sounds vaguely reminiscent of the Nixon administration,
it should.) Would it not be within the realm of possibility that one day the sleeping American masses could
awaken and find the last semblance of their democracy
gone? Even with a small "attentive public" the risk of
such a scenario's occurring is too great for us to be
willing to settle for "elite" democracy.

Even if there were no such risk, I would still
find such limited aspirations for democracy objection-
able. After all, democracy means that the people rule,
and to do this the people must be in the act. Unless a
man is going to be actively involved in the process of
participating in those governmental decisions that
affect him--and they all do--you have something less
than the promise of democracy. True, if large numbers
of the American public in their present state suddenly
began to take a really active role in their government,
they would in all likelihood louse things up. However,
if we were able to substantially increase the number of
responsible citizens, there is no reason to think that
things would not be better. This would not be your
"ugly American" suddenly jumping into the fray with
both left feet, but rather a greatly increased number
of people who would understand the system, understand
the issues, and would take reasoned action on matters
of government. Surely this would more nearly approach
the promise of representative democracy, and, unless
there is nothing at all to basic democratic theory, an
improved form of government would emerge. So, as you
knew I would, I contend that it is desirable that we
attempt to greatly expand the number of responsible

citizens in the U.S.

Now, we return to the question, Can it really be done? No one actually knows. I'll take a look with you at the prospects and then, as you know I will, conclude that it can be done--but it's going to turn out to be a mighty "iffy" yes.

I am certain that we can develop citizens that have a good understanding of their government. We can produce people that understand the history, philosophy, structure and mechanics of representative democracy. Further, we can see to it that these citizens are fully aware of the dissonance that exists between the present operation of government and the text book description of democracy. We know how to do this kind of thing. That we haven't done it doesn't mean that we can't; it just means that we haven't.

In like manner we can produce a citizen that has an in-depth understanding of the basic tenets of democracy. We can see to it that he knows in very specific ways such things as the meaning of the basic rights and freedoms--as well as the responsibilities-- of an American citizen. Whether we can enlist his strong support for these kinds of things is another matter. About the best I can predict is a "definite maybe." When we shift out of the area of skills and knowledge, we move into an area of education in which there is considerably more heat than light. It has never ceased to amaze me, that despite all of our talk about the importance of developing attutudes and values, we know very little about how to do it. I , of course have some very definite ideas about how to go about the development of attitudes and values which I will deal with in subsequent chapters. In any event, unlike the good grasp we have on the techniques of teaching skills and imparting information (regardless of whether we do what we know or not), when we contemplate the means of developing attitudes and values we enter an educational swamp. Perhaps, then, we can develop citizens who really support the foundational ideas of democracy. Perhaps.

What about the possibility of producing a citizen who will keep himself informed? Is is even possible for any citizen to stay informed? It isn't uncommon to read or hear that the matters of government have become so complicated that it is impossible for anyone other than an expert to comprehend them. If one is so inclined this serves as a beautiful excuse for not

bothering to try. It also can be used as a basis for
governmental leaders, bureaucrats, and "experts" to
decide that, since we couldn't understand anyway, they
won't bother to try and explain. From this it is only
a small step to the idea that what we don't know won't
hurt us and from there to the excessive governmental
secrecy we have experienced with ever-increasing frequency. (In this latter regard, I've about concluded
that the only people the American government effectively keeps secrets from are the American people.) While
no one can doubt that some of the issues that confront
our government at any given time are exceedingly complex, this does not mean that these issues can't be
understood by ordinary persons. Even if the details
might be beyond the grasp of the average citizens,
surely the basic principles involved would not be beyond comprehension. Perhaps if our government expended
the energy it uses trying to keep things from us in
attempting to explain things to us, we could understand
them. (The obvious exception to this is the inflation
problem which apparently no one understands.) Actually,
most of the basic issues aren't all that complicated
anyway, and salient problems can be comprehended if
one will just learn to follow them as they develop
day by day. I think it is entirely possible for citizens to be taught techniques of staying informed that,
with some government cooperation, would allow them to
stay abrest of issues. Whether we can persuade our
citizenry that they ought to use these techniques is
another question. Again when we encounter this matter
of attitude, we must recognize that knowing how to do
it sure as heck isn't the same thing as doing it.

Over the years a number of approaches have been
developed that have been reasonably successful in
teaching the skills of critical thinking. For years
the techniques of inquiry training, deductive reasoning,
and propaganda analysis have been available in forms
that can be used with school children. More recently
an approach to formal logic has been developed for use
with these youngsters. As is the case with other
skills, we have fairly satisfactory means of teaching
them. That we haven't had widespread use of this material is obvious. In the main we seem to have made
the erroneous assumption that by teaching a kid the
"scientific method" in some science class we have en-
abled him to practice critical thinking in all matters.
Slips! Nonetheless, we have available to us the vehicles through which we can teach the skills of the
critical thinking process. Once more then, the basic
problem isn't can we teach him how, but will he use

what he knows?

Finally we come to the matter of the possibility of developing a citizen who will participate. This is the real tough one because it is practically all a matter of attitude. After all, while the subject can't be ignored, there isn't a whole lot involved in teaching someone how to participate. (That is, if you happen to know how yourself.) The hitch is to get him to do it. And, what makes this really sticky is the fact that it is highly possible for a reasonable person--a critical thinker if you will--to conclude that his participation in the democratic process doesn't make sense. It is not unreasonable for a person to decide that his participation in many ways doesn't make any difference, because in many ways it doesn't. Small wonder that the efficacy studies cited earlier weren't more encouraging. To be a responsible citizen takes time and effort. I don't think it requires an inordinate amount, but it does take time and effort to stay informed about the issues that confront your government. There is no question that thinking, particularly critical thinking, is time consuming and hard work. (Perhaps this explains in part why we human beings do so precious little of it.) Even at a minimal level, it takes time and effort to participate. So, if you should happen to take a hard look at the huge size and remote nature of your government and recognize how insignificant you are when massed with the great number of your fellow citizens, it is possible to conclude that your time and effort will not make one bit of difference. At this point, one will be hard put to convince you that you should do your "good citizen" thing and participate. Let George do it. Unless you can be convinced that there are compelling reasons for your participation that override this conclusion, you're not going to expend the time and effort. I doubt that you would be swayed by the argument--true though it may be--that if everyone took your attitude the whole "democratic process" would go down the tube. Maybe if we can teach you ways in which you, by yourself or through groups, can be more effective, we can encourage you to participate. Maybe not. Perhaps if we can show you examples in which one person has made a difference, it will help. One thing is for sure: unless we can find some way to equip you with a psychological override that will give you compelling reason to participate, despite the good reasons for not doing so, you are going to sit back with the majority of your fellow Americans and ignore the whole political schmeer. Somehow we must build into as many citizens

as possible the sentiment expressed in this bit of
verse by Bonaro Overstreet:

Stubborn Ounces

(To One Who Doubts the Worth of Doing
Anything if You Can't Do Everything)

You say the little efforts that I make
will do no good: they never will prevail
to tip the hovering scale
where Justice hangs in the balance.
                                    I don't think
I ever thought they would.
But I am prejudiced beyond debate
in favor of my right to choose which side
shall feel the stubborn ounces of my weight.[4]

As I said earlier, I think it possible to produce a substantial number of individuals who will meet
the criteria of responsible citizenship. I do indeed
believe it's possible. I also believe that it is essential that it be tried. But, in all candor, even
under the best of conditions, it is going to be most
difficult. If it were easy, it would have already
been accomplished. And, this brings me to the topic
of the next chapter.

---

[4]Overstreet, Bonaro W., Signature: New and Selected Poems,
"Stubborn Ounces," 1978, W.W. Norton. Reprinted by permission of
W.W.Norton, Publisher.

WHY HASN'T IT HAPPENED?

I'm tempted to just say it hasn't happened because no one has much wanted it to and let it go at that. Short chapter. While I really do believe that this is the reason, I think it requires at least some explanation. While they all end up at the same place, there are several threads of thought that I want to trace in explaining why we haven't produced many responsible citizens.

In the preceding chapter I pretty well established the background for the first reason, which is that we really haven't made a serious effort in public education to get this particular job done. There are a number of casual factors that explain why this has been the case, which I will deal with in a moment. As I pointed out, we have effective ways of presenting information and teaching skills. No, we don't succeed with every individual--neither does any other vocation--but with most of them we know how to get these jobs done. Knowing this, the fact that we have produced so few citizens that understand the system and can think rationally, is _prima facie_ evidence that we haven't done much more than give lip service to citizenship education. While we don't know a lot about the business of developing attitudes, this is not to be taken to mean that we know nothing about it. Other than a vague positive attitude toward the good old U.S. of America, which we may or may not have had anything to do with, there is little evidence of our successfully developing "good" citizenship attitudes.

For many years I worked in the public schools. For all of my adult life I have not been far removed from them. I know what it is like when public school teachers get serious about something. When it comes to citizenship education, the evidence of this seriousness of purpose is not to be found. Of course you can find a teacher here and a school there, that is"with the program," but they are the exception. In the main, citizenship education is given a lick and a promise and a lot of lip service. The program, the example, and environment that might--just might--produce responsible citizens is, in most cases, glaringly absent. The schools and the people who work in them are not really committed to this task. The reason they aren't is that there is no real support for them to be so committed and considerable pressure for them not to be.

The vocation of teaching in the United States--and the world for that matter--has a long history of dedication. Of this teachers can be proud. But, we do not have a history that presents many examples of teacher courage. In the main, we have been a vocation that is peopled by those who do what they are told to do. While we have from time to time subverted directives by just being apathetic about them, our most predominate modus operandi have been to comply with orders, yield to pressures, and bow to authority--at least to outward appearance. There appear to be two major factors that explain this characteristic of the teaching "profession." First, as I mentioned earlier, societies set up educational systems for the purpose of perpetuating themselves. Having established such a system, the powers that be are seldom if ever willing to relinquish control of it. On the contrary, invariably the educational system is kept under close supervision to insure that those who are attempting to influence the future will do it in ways that are approved by the powers that be. So it is that the history of teaching is filled to overflowing with examples of the minute control that communities and governing bodies have exercised over not only the professional life, but the personal life of teachers. With this kind of history, and a legal structure that serves to perpetuate it, the vocation of teaching, until recently, seldom attracted and rapidly expelled the kinds of individuals that possessed a spirit of independence and courage. Studies show that the spawning ground of most teachers is the upper-lower and lower-middle socio-economic class.[1] These individuals are upwardly mobile with aspirations for achieving the middle class status they believe school teachers occupy. (Only too late do they come to know the "quiet desperation in genteel poverty" that

---

[1]For more detailed discussions of the background and history of school teachers as an occupational group, see: Myron Brenton, What's Happened to Teacher? New York, Avon Books, 1970, pp. 28-77. Harmon Zeigler, The Political Life of American Teachers, Englewood Cliffs, N.H., Prentice-Hall, 1967, pp. 31-44. Dan C. Lortie, School Teacher, A Sociological Study, Chicago, The University of Chicago Press, 1975, pp. 1-54.

more adequately describes the lot of the school marm and master.) Such individuals are ripe for the pressure to conform that one who teaches will immediately encounter. Until the most recent past, and even then only ever so slightly, it was safe to assume that school teachers would do as they were told. Such being the case, they were not going to get really serious about developing responsible citizens unless someone told them to do so. (Under the circumstances it would have probably been impossible anyway. As Harold Benjamin said, "Free men cannot be taught properly by slaves. Courageous citizens cannot be well educated by scared hired men."[2]) Surely without outside support for the education of effective citizens, there would be no concerted effort in the public schools to accomplish this task. There has been no support for doing this, and there has been pressure against it. Now, let me clarify this. You and I both know that there has been a great deal of support for our teaching "good citizenship" and from time to time considerable public clamor for our fostering more patriotism. That, however, is not what I'm talking about. I'm talking about support for the development of the kind of responsible citizen I have described over and again in this book. And, I submit to you that the pressure for us to do this kind of a job has been conspicuous by its absence. Why?

Why? Because nobody much wants it. Let's take a look at several of the customary sources of support and/or pressure that might work their influence on the schools and on teachers.

We can immediately write off school administrators and school boards, whose primary concerns in the citizenship area are that we operate schools with a minimum of conflict and disruption. Likewise we can eliminate prospective employers, who, if they have any concern at all, are more interested in our producing people who can carry out instructions, than in our developing responsible citizens.

What of the parents? Don't they want us to turn

---

[2]This is on a poster distributed by the National Education Association Commission on Professional Right and Responsibilities and is attributed to the late Dr. Harold Benjamin who was a member of the NEA Defense Commission and a professor at George Peabody College in Nashville, Tennessee.

their offspring into responsible citizens? Not particularly. We must remember that the parents are also
the poor citizens we have been describing. While it is
probably true that they want things to be better for
their children, when they say "better" they are talking
about more loot and not about better citizenship. Citizenship is not a central concern in their lives, and
there is no reason to think it will be of high priority in their thoughts about the lives of their children. Besides, what father wants some child around him
who practices critical thinking, or is better informed,
or is an activist? Better the kid keep his nose clean
and be a star athlete or cheerleader. No, there hasn't
been and there isn't going to be a major ground swell
among the parents that forces us to get about our good
citizen business.

How about those community leaders--the influenc-
tial citizens, the group labeled the power structure--
the people in our town, our state, our nation who
really run things? (Let me pause here to state that I
believe a power structure will exist in any social
structure that exists. Always there will be those
among us that exert a disproportionate amount of influence on the decision-making process. I do not view
this as some kind of conspiracy through which a few
individuals plot and scheme to work their will on the
rest of us. Rather, power structures are simply a
community of interest amoung those who, usually on the
basis of substantial financial resources, occupy positions of great influence. What these people appear to
have in common is a desire to protect and expand their
financial interests. Rare indeed is the power figure
who has a genuine concern for us peons.) No, the power
structure has not used, and will not use, its influence
to cause the public schools to increase the output of
responsible citizens. After all, a greatly expanded,
enlightened citizenry would in all likelihood result in
a great reduction in the influence of the powerful few.
This is a development that few power figures would wel-
come or encourage. Far better to have a populace that
is ignorant, gullible, unconcerned, and uninvolved.
Under these circumstances it is far easier to run
things in such a way as to insure the continued financial aggrandizement of the powerful, even if it is to
the detriment of the masses.

Well then, can we look for support from those
who are actively involved in the political process, the
politicians, the elected officials? Heck no. They may
be many many things, but rare indeed is the politician

that is suicidal. Think for a moment of the politicians, the elected officials, with whom you are familiar. Now think about the kind of responsible citizen I have been talking about. How long do you think such a citizen would permit the average office holder to remain an incumbent? The last thing in the world that your average politician wants is an enlightened, rational and active electorate. What he wants to do is to continue to spout platitudes about being proud to be a servant of, by, and for the people. What he wants is a euphoric mass of people who will stay the hell out of things while he and his cronies perpetuate themselves in office. Support from the run-of-the-mill politician for an effective program of citizenship education? Never!

Perhaps we could look to the news media for support. On the basis of absolutely no hard evidence, I have the feeling that most of the people in the media are supportive of the basic tenets of democracy. I have this feeling that at the working press level, perhaps even at the editorial level, the people of the media would like to see us more nearly approach the promise of representative democracy. Perhaps this is just one more personal pipe dream. If, however, this "gut feeling" of mine is correct, the media might be a source of potential support. To this point though, except in the form of vague, general, and usually shallow exhortations, no real pressure has come from the media.

This brings us back, full circle, to those of us who teach.

First let's look at the college professors who from time to time have pointed out that we haven't exactly enjoyed spectacular success as citizen producers. Having arrived at this conclusion, they have, on occasion, suggested ways and given encouragement that they felt would lead to improvement. As is often the case in many fields, the diagnosis of the problem was frequently superior to the prescribed cure. More often than not, as is true in most instances where college professors turn their attention to public education, these efforts resulted in much more debate among the academicians than in practical consequences in the practices of school teachers. (At this point it no doubt occurs to you to wonder why I think my efforts are going to turn out any differently. I don't know. I just hope that they will.) If we college teachers can learn to avoid the practice of using our studies of the work of the public school teachers as a basis for

79

fulfilling our need to assert our own insecurely held feeling of superiority, we can perhaps be a source of support to public education. To this point most of us college professors would be more aptly described as part of the problem rather than part of the solution.

Finally, we return to the public school teachers. In the absence of any real support, we have treated citizenship education in an off-handed fashion that practically guaranteed our failure. (I want to reiterate that there have been exceptions of individual teachers and occasionally a rare school in which conscientious and effective work has been done. It is, by the way, the awareness of these exceptions that encourages me to continue to believe that such success is possible on a large scale.) In the process of failing, we in public education have developed a definition of good citizenship for school children that, in terms of representative democracy, defies understanding. Think, if you will, of what we in the school business are talking about when we refer to a student as being a "good citizen." Right! He is the kid who knows what is expected of him, does what he is told, and doesn't rock the boat. Okay, way back in Chapter 3 when I repeated it, you knew this was coming. This concept of good citizenship is that which is compatible with the definition of a responsible citizen in a totalitarian system, not a democracy. This definition of citizenship is really only symptomatic of an entire approach to children that, no matter what else might have occurred, would have insured our inability to get the job done.

For all of these reasons we have failed. If we are to turn this failure into success, it will require that we teachers, with little outside support, undertake the near impossible task of doing it. This will require that we school teachers see the need to do this. To this point, this is what I have tried to establish in your mind. Beyond this we will also need to see the way and find the courage. It is to these two tasks that I will now turn my attention.

THE THEORY

For several years now I have taught "theory"
courses to graduate students. On the basis of this
experience, I think the first thing I'd better do is
write out a disclaimer. It is <u>not</u> necessary that theory
be useless, difficult, and obscure. On the contrary,
there is nothing more practical than sound theory: it
can serve as a basis and guideline for effective practice. It is in this context that I have titled this
chapter "The Theory." In this chapter I'm going to
state those things that I believe about human learning
that are reflected in the chapters that follow.

I'm not going to do a lot of name-dropping in
this chapter nor am I going to cite a stack of studies.
For those of you who might care, you will find my position heavy laden with the thinking of the philosopher
John Dewey, as I understand his writings, and the psy-
chologist Art Combs, as I understood his teaching. At
first blush this may appear an unlikely combination,
but, since I am less scientifically oriented than the
Pragmatist Dewey and less inclined toward Existential-
ism than the Humanist Combs, my position seems--at
least to me--to be plausible.

I believe that there is some sort of life force
in each human being. Whether you think of this force
as the drive to survive that is implicit in all the
works of Dewey or the drive to adequacy that is ex-
plicit in all the writings of Combs, it still seems to
exist. To try to explain human behavior and ignore this
force is to ignore the realities of human behavior.
Right from the start there is some drive--some force--
that keeps us humans hanging in there trying to cope,
to adjust, to handle, to survive. Were this not the
case, why would we bother? It is the assumption of the
existence of this life force that gives validity to the
contention of Abraham Maslow that there is a heirarchy
of human needs that must be met in order of their priority. First, according to Maslow, are the survival
needs which must be met before other needs, less crucial than physical survival, can even be entertained.

Call it what you may, there is in every human being a force that makes him more than just the sum of his past experiences. He has a drive to stay alive.

While we are well advised to be very tentative about stating what a human being is, we can say with certainty that he exists in an evironment that is constantly changing. Unless this human being can interact with this changing environment in a satisfactory manner, he will fall by the wayside. In the most extreme evolutionary form, this can be described as "adjust or perish." So it is that if an individual is going to survive--physically and psychologically--he must make adequate adjustment to his changing environment. Other human beings will constitute that aspect of his environment to which he will most frequently need to adjust. (As did Dewey, I use the word adjust in the active not passive sense in which individuals adjust their environment to themselves as well as adjust to the environment. This interaction with the changing environment is sometimes known as 'problem solving.')

Until he dies, a human being is not a finished product. (I'll leave the matter of what happens to him after death to the theologians.) It is more sound to think of a human being as a point in process. Thus at any given time he is a stage in the process of interacting with his changing environment. He brings to this point of interaction his life force, his native ability (whatever that means), his self concept, and his past experience of interacting with his environment. Granted, the particular environment in which he finds himself will influence the kinds of adjustments that are open to him. In this regard it is of vital importance for an individual to know the constraints and limits of the environment in which he finds himself. However, insofar as he can, the individual human being is constantly selecting from his environment those things to which he will attempt to adjust.

The individual human being deals with those things in his environment that are important and interesting to him and those that he feels that he is capable of dealing with. If something in his environment is unimportant or uninteresting to him, he will ignore it, or if motivated to deal with it though some secondary source, he will soon discard and forget it. If he is not capable of dealing with something, he will withdraw from it, ignore it, distort it, or avoid it. Failing in all of these tactics, he will become immobilized in the face of it. An individual functions best when the problem that confronts him is a challenge to him--one not so easy as to bore him and not so difficult as to threaten him.

The better an individual feels about himself--the more positive his self concept--and the more his background is filled with success in coping with past problems, the greater will be the likelihood that he will have effective interaction with his present environment. While there are certain understandings and certain skills that can help an individual make adequate adjustments, the crucial factor is the attitude with which he approaches the interaction.

While each human being is unique in his self concept and past experience, there are enough similarities in human needs and enough potential for shared experience through communication that it is possible to anticipate that humans will have some common understandings, skills, and attitudes. It appears that it is possible, through deliberate effort, to enlarge this common ground. While it is important to keep in mind the unique individuality of each human being, it is equally vital to remember the commonality they share.

When a young human being enters school, he already knows how to learn, is ready to continue the process, and is usually eager to get on with it. More often than not, the reality of school falls short of his expectations. If, on entering school, he could continue to function in terms of his own immediate goals and interests, chances are that he would never lose his enthusiasm for learning--even in the school setting.

We in the schools need to recognize that, in the main, a kid is going to learn on his own terms. That is, he is going to function on the basis of those things that are important to him--his own goals and interests. When we deal with him on his terms, we function on the basis of "primary motivation," and can expect him to learn well. Through the use of rewards, loss of privileges, punishment, and other techniques of "secondary motivation," we can move a child to learn some things, but the result is shallow and fleeting. We may not like the idea that these little human beings honestly feel that their concerns and priorities are more pressing then those we seek to impose on them, but it is nonetheless the way things are.

This doesn't make them perverse, it makes them human.
Like it or not, this is the way things are, and we err
when we fail to take this principle of learning into
account.

Society, on the other hand, is not and will not
be content to let a child remain aloof from school or
move through school operating solely on the basis of
his own immediate needs. There are things--knowledge
and skills--that society feels he must know if he is to
function effectively in the social order. More often
than not, these things--the expectations of society--
are long range and remote from immediate application
to the goals and interests of the child. Here then is
where the rub comes. There is usually a wide gap between the immediate goals and interests of the kid, his
reality, and the requirements of the school. In my
judgment, most of the problems that occur in school can
be found to ultimately stem from this dislocation.
When the activities required of a youngster are foreign
to his reality, you can anticipate that his learning
will be inefficient and short lived, or he will develop techniques with which he avoids or withdraws from
the task at hand. Under such circumstances, it appears
that learning--at least the formal requirements of
learning that they encounter in society's educational
institutions--is a terrible drag. This is a sad com-
mentary. As children move through the stages of formal
schooling, we seem to manage to stifle their almost ir-
repressible urge to learn. Even so, we do not completely succeed. Even those who believe that they are in-
capable of learning in school still remain effective
learners when dealing with matters that are relevant to
their own goals and interests. For example, the school
dropouts who have mastered the complexities of auto
mechanics, surfing, salesmanship, etc.

This, then is the basic principle of teaching:
A student will learn best those things that are presented to him in such a way as to be directly related
to his immediate interests and goals.

Now this principle does not necessarily imply
undertaking that which was once known as the "child-
centered curriculum." What this does require is that
we approach kids with the things we feel are important
for them to learn in such a way that they can make immediate application of them to their lives. In this
regard it is well to keep in mind that young people
have tremendous curiosity and when properly approached
can be interested in practically anything. Obviously

the most effective way to approach them is in terms of
direct application to the immediate reality of their
lives. When such an approach is neither possible nor
practical, the next most promising approach is through
simulation or role playing. However, it should be kept
in mind that this, at best, is an avenue that is a very
poor second. The least effective approach to the development of interest is secondary motivation through
the artificial goals of rewards, withdrawal of privi-
lege, and punishment.

In all teaching it is imperative that those
things we ask of children be within their grasp.
Learning is most productive and effective when that
which is expected of a child is neither so easy as to
bore him nor so difficult as to threaten him. The key
is to have the youngster deal with things that are a
challenge to him--to undertake the solutions to problems which will make him reach, but which are within
his grasp. Nothing will more greatly enhance the continued development of an effective learner than a long
succession of successful efforts at dealing with situations that are neither too difficult nor too easy
for him.

That which a child experiences through the actual application of his own solution to a problem which
is significant to him will result in a quality of
learning that is superior to other kinds. This is another way of stating Dewey's truism that we learn best
that which we directly experience. This does not mean
that there is no place in education for vicarious experience, mental trial and error, and abstract thinking. Nor does it mean that we need a spate of random
activity in the name of "learning by doing." What it
does mean is that we human beings derive meaning from
the consequences of our acts. The more direct the connection between our act and its consequences, the
better the learning.

If a kid in school is going to experience the
authentic consequences of the application of a solution
he develops to some problem, he must be free to make
mistakes. Obviously the range of possible mistakes
open to him must be limited in terms of his maturation
so as to rule out errors that would do damage to him
and/or harm to others. Taking into consideration this
one caution, we should recognize that each child needs
to have open to him for decision making as wide a range
of choices as can possibly be afforded.

As a child progresses through school, changes--
physical, intellectual, emotional--occur in him. We
sometimes refer to this process as "maturation." It is
important that teachers give this the recognition that
it deserves and adjust their approach to children in
terms of this maturation process. The quantity and
complexity of choices open to students should increase
as they progress through school. When a school deals
with its seniors in essentially the same fashion as it
does it first-graders, it is not taking this maturation
process into account.

I know that you do not teach an individual to
assume responsibility for himself by requiring of him
that he do those things that we feel are "responsible."
From the earliest days of education we have tried the
"habituation" approach, and it has consistently failed
us. We may want to believe that we can build good
lifetime habits into individuals by making them do
things our way over and over again--we may even want
to believe that such unpleasant activity strengthens
their moral fiber--but it just isn't true. This I know.
I think an individual learns to be responsible for himself by being responsible for himself, by being able
to make choices, act on these choices, and encounter
the consequences of these actions.

There will be, of course, some information that
teachers will feel is vital for a child to know. In
all likelihood there will also be some things that,
needed or not, society will expect the school to in-
culate. In this instance it is probable that society
will continue to expect that some things be learned
early by rote. In cases where we are obliged to resort
to rote learning with those who are too inexperienced
to comprehend the meaning of the words and phrases they
are committing to memory, let us do so with the inflex-
ible determination to review the meaning of these
things at a later time when they can be understood.

While the schools can be helpful in providing
information that a child may need, and in teaching him
skills that he will very likely need, the really important contributions that a school can make to an individual is in the realm of attitudes. I realize that
this flies in the face of much educational practice.
Even though we profess our concern with the primacy of
attitude development, our practice centers around the
distribution of information and the development of
skills. This is probably the result of our circumstances, in which we find that it is much easier to

impart information and practice skills than it is to develop attitudes. This fact, that we don't do what we say, in no way detracts from the crucial significance of attitude development.

In the matter of attitudes, first and foremost is the development of an essentially positive self concept. This is the one single, crucial attitude factor. With it much can follow. Without it little of good will ensue. Kids arrive at school, of course, with some sort of self concept. While the extent to which the school can influence self concept is debatable, that the school can inflence it is not. Surely if throughout a school an individual is treated in terms of the dignity and worth that is inherent in every human being, it cannot harm and will in all likelihood enhance his self concept. Further it seems reasonable to assume that a school that provides him with a steady progression of authentic success in dealing with problems that challenge him will do much to aid the development of a positive view of self. This self concept will be even more likely developed if he is in an atmosphere where it is acceptable to think for himself, put his thoughts into action, encounter the consequences and make errors.

Of almost equal importance is the development of an attitude that recognizes the worth and dignity of others. That the development of such an attitude is contingent on a positive self concept is so well recognized that it constitutes a truism. These two attitudes, a positive self concept and the appreciation of the dignity and worth of others, are not only essential to the development of an adequate human being, they are basic in the maintenance of a democracy.

We really don't know a heck of a lot about the development of attitudes and values, but this is not to be taken to mean that we know nothing. In fact we do know some things. For instance, we have good reason to believe that the approach taken to children by teachers, particularly the recognition of their dignity and worth, can and does make a difference in how they see themselves. After all, we derive much of our understanding of ourselves from the reactions we elicit from others. More important than the approach we take to children is the example we set for them. The example of what the pyschologists term a "significant other"--in this case the teacher--can work considerable influence on a kid's attitude. This continues to be true even through adolescence when a young person is so responsive to his peer group. The example lived that reinforces the words that are spoken, rather than gives lie to them, is particularly effective as an influence on attitudes. Finally, of equal importance to the example demonstrated is the environment provided. If certain attitudes are to be inculcated, it is vital that the environment support in every way the development of these attitudes. If the messages that an individual receives from his environment are contrary to the desired attitudes and values, it is a counter productive situation. Thus, specific attention must be given to the approach, the example, and the environment because they are all of great importance in the development of attitudes. If the development of a desired attitude is to be effective, it is necessary that the precept taught must be reinforced by the approach to the student, the example set for him, and the environment in which he finds himself.

Now all that has preceded this most certainly doesn't constitute a full blown essay on the nature of man, nor is it a complete philosophy of education. What it does represent is a description of the principles that served to guide my thinking as I set out to develop my ideas about schools that can produce responsible citizens. As you read through this material, I doubt that you found anything that was particularly startling to you. In the main, these principles represent an ordering--a listing--of those "truths" that those of us who have spent years teaching have learned from our experience. True, some of those things we do know to do, we implement poorly or not at all. Why our actual practice so frequently falls short of that which we know to be the best educational principles is not particularly relevant here and, save for points where it is applicable in later chapters, will be left to other authors. Suffice it to say that we know how to teach better than we actually do. Even so, the program I will now set forth is based on that which I believe to.be the best we know about how to teach.

THE KNOWLEDGE

There are those who can make a good case that
there are no specific items of knowledge that are essential for a person to function effectively in society.
In part I agree with them. At least I agree with them
to the point of acknowledging that in this world of
such rapid change, it is impossible to know at any
given time what someone will need to know at a later
time. However, this does not mean that it is impossible to make some pretty good guesses. What this
really means to me is that it is much more important to
try to provide a human being with the skills and
attitudes that will enable him to learn whatever it is
that he will need to know rather than to guess what
information he will need. Certainly there is no particular magic residing in certain subject matter that
will enable us, once having mastered it, to adequately
cope with all aspects of our future. While the possession of information that is generally held to constitute an "education" will no doubt provide an individual with a certain amount of security and opportunity it may or may not serve him well in dealing
with the future problems. This is not to say that the
acquisition of particular information, or knowledge,
isn't important, but rather that it is not as important as the development of the skills and attitudes of
effective learning. It would be foolish to contend,
particularly as it relates to the development of responsible citizens that all knowledge is of equal importance. And, certainly it would be ridiculous to
submit that the acquisition of knowledge is of no consequence at all. Further, even if this were not the case,
subject matter, or information, is the medium through
which the skills of learning are mastered. Inasmuch as
subject matter must be used to develop skills, you may
as well try to select that information which you guess
will be of greatest value to the individual. So,
granting as essentially correct the idea that an individual with the skills and attitudes that would cause
him to want to be a good citizen, would in all likelihood learn those things he needed to know, let's see
what kind of information we could give him that would

likely provide a headstart.

I think I earlier conveyed my attitude regarding rote learning, so let's get it out of the way first. Meaningless or not, there are some things that society will require, or expect us, to "teach" the children early in their educational life. OK, there is no particular harm in this. However, if these kinds of things are of the significance that society seems to assign to them, they may well be worth understanding. So, let's resolve that when the students can, we will deliberately see if we can help them understand the meaning of those things they have memorized earlier. For example, somewhere around the sixth or seventh grade let's take a little time and explain to the kids what they are saying, and why they are reciting the "Pledge to the Flag." About that same time let's spend some time talking about what was going on when Francis Scott Key wrote the National Anthem, and what it all means. The same should be done with the other songs and words they memorize, and the symbols they encounter before they can possibly grasp their meaning. This is not a "big deal" thing that has to be made a major production but is rather just something we need to remember to take care of.

With three additions, I think those things that we have traditionally thought to be important information in the development of a responsible citizen still are. Certainly it is helpful to a responsible citizen to know the historical development of his form of government in both the world and his own country, to understand the basic documents on which his government is based, to grasp the structure and mechanics of his form of government, and to be familiar with the issues and problems that confront his society at any given time. All of these things have in the past been considered important in the public schools.

Regarding these things, then, the challenge is to develop more effective ways of teaching them. To the above listing I would add the need to understand the basic philosophy of democracy, the need to have a comparative understanding of democracy as it relates to other forms of government, and, most importantly, the need to understand the realities of our government as it is practiced. These three things have seldom been done in public education so the challenge is both to do them and do them well.

In the matter of teaching the history of

democracy and developing an understanding of the great documents that mark its advancement, I don't have a lot to offer for the first few years of a child's education. I do know that there are those who presently find ways to bring this material to life for children. I suppose that until a child is old enough to grasp abstract ideas and causal relationships the chronological approach is as good as any. For those teachers who cannot manage to bring to history the enthusiasm and vitality it deserves, I'd suggest the liberal use of the many fine audio and visual and audio-visual materials that are available for this subject. It would also seem to me that the teaching of these concepts of history is greatly enhanced by use of specific examples from contemporary life, particularly the life of the kids you are teaching.

Once a child can comprehend abstract ideas and the concept of cause and effect, I think history should be taught backwards. By this, I mean that we should deal with history by tracing the causal roots of contemporary problems. I realize that this doesn't allow a teacher to organize the subject matter into nice neat packages. In fact this "backwards" approach doesn't even guarantee that specified subject matter will be covered at all. Such an approach would no doubt cross time lines and continental borders in a fashion that would raise havoc with the present day organization of social studies subject matter. While the chronological coverage of the subject matter in early grades would perhaps compensate a little for this, there would no doubt be great gaps in the coverage of historical data. Personally I'm willing to sacrifice this if in the process we can develop youngsters that can actually see the relationship between the conditions of the present and the events of the past. If we adopt such an approach, it would require that our high school courses change from "history of..." or the "...period," to "problems of...." Actually I have worked in schools where this has been done. Such an approach requires a re-orientation of the teachers, a major adjustment on the part of most parents and a minor accommodation on the part of most students. It seems to work, or so the teachers told me. In truth I imagine the gaps this approach leaves are not nearly as great as we suspect, and the coverage under our present approach is not nearly as comprehensive and lasting as we might think. So, rather than the present offering of an occasional optional course of this nature, most of our secondary school social studies would take the form of Problems in American Democracy with the clear understanding that this would include the problems of the school, the community, the state, the nation, and the world. Surely such an approach would inevitably provide a student with a thorough knowledge of the history of the development of democracy, an awareness of the significant documents on which it's based, and an understanding of what it implies in today's world. In this I'm not assuming that the study of today's problems and their historical roots will, through some magic, cause kids to learn of these things I just listed. I simply don't see how you can approach the subject matter in this fashion without encountering this information. Further, I surmise that such an approach would greatly enhance the possibility that the information so encountered, would be seen to have application to the realities of today.

In our efforts to develop a citizen who can, and will, stay well informed about the problems and issues that confront his government, we start strong and finish poorly. By this I mean that the practice of dealing each day with significant current events is the proper approach to this aspect of citizenship education. That we do this in the elementary years is an accepted fact. That we fail to do this beyond the elementary years is equally obvious. I think this is an error. Once we move beyond the self-contained, or semi-self-contained classroom and into the compart-mentalized, subject-centered secondary school, current events become nobody's business. True, occasionally you can find a course on current events--usually in a school that is involved in a phase elective program-- but this is not the day-by-day everyday dealing with current events that I'm talking about. Now, I want to make it clear that I advocate this for reasons other than the development of good habits. If "good habits" of staying informed should happen to result from the practice of deliberately dealing with current events on an everyday basis, that's great. But, I'm not going to base my case on these doubtful grounds. Rather, there are three other reasons why I advocate that we continue to deal regularly with current issues and problems through all the years of formal schooling. First, this will provide us with the vehicle through which we can teach kids how to stay well informed. (It will also give us a really good means to develop the skills of critical thinking with which I will deal in the next chapter.) Actually, the key to staying well informed about issues and problems of government is to do it on a regular basis. Thus, in this instance we can, in a very direct fashion, provide our students with the opportunity to learn this by actually doing it. Well, you say, isn't this exactly what we have been doing in the elementary grades? Yes, I answer, but... the "but" being that changes occur in the kids right around the time we stop this practice, and they really don't get any experience in doing it at an adult level. This, then, is a prime reason for continuing to maintain this practice through the period when a student becomes capable of dealing with abstraction and cause and effect. Closely related to this reason is my second point in support of such a program, which is example that it sets. By persisting in this practice throughout the entire span of school years, we convey to our charges the clear message that we think this practice is important. In this regard, I think it essential that we establish this practice in such a way as to involve most, if not all, of our secondary teachers. It would be a real mistake, in this matter of example-setting, to develop a program that would relegate this activity to the social studies teachers. In schools that have homerooms, the matter of current events could be dealt·with during the homeroom period. Homeroom could easily be scheduled in such a way as to provide adequate time for this activity, and, in many instances, it would constitute a great improvement over what is presently being done. Having spent several years scheduling schools, I know that no matter what other factors may be involved, time can be arranged to take care of this activity if it is really considered important. An it is important. The final reason I advocate this approach is that it has the potential for building a base for understanding future problems. Rarely, if ever, does a social issue develop full-blown overnight. More than likely it evolves over a long period of time with the issue or problem of the moment, being, in fact, a single aspect of a continuing condition. Such being the case, the practice of following the development of issues will in all likelihood stand a person in good stead throughout his lifetime as he encounters specific problems that emerge from them. Surely it will give him a chance to understand the context in which the problem of the moment exists. All in all such an approach will show an individual how to stay informed, provide him with a base of understanding from which he can continue to be informed, show him that it is considered important, and demostrate to him that it is not as difficult to do as he might otherwise imagine.

Now to the matter of helping a youngster understand the structure of his government. It really came as a shock to me that we haven't been particularly successful in this. I had truly assumed that we would have produced at least a populace in which more than half of the people are aware that each state has two United States Senators. Sigh. In the main this should be just a matter of imparting straight-forward, fairly simple information. This is what we are supposed to do best. Apparently this stuff comes in the category of that which kids learn and forget or never learn at all because we somehow fail to get it to them in a form, and at a time, when it is of any real significance to them. Perhaps some of the things I'm going to suggest in the later chapters will help to create conditions where the relevance of this information will be more apparent to the students. Beyond this, it might help alleviate this condition if we see to it that the structure of our government (governments) is seen as being directly related to what is going on today. By this I mean that, while it is important to know of the drafting of the U.S. Constitution in 1783, or the adoption of the Bill of Rights, or the circumstances under which other amendments have come and gone, it is of much greater significance to know these things, as former Senator Sam Ervin knows them, in terms of what they mean today. Again, if we can approach our study of these things from the perspective of current problems, we can in all likelihood increase the possibility of their being seen as having immediate relevance. Further, I think we can contribute to a better understanding of the structure and organization of our governments if we deliberately show the kids the discrepancy that exists between the way government is supposed to work and the way it is actually working. Surely it can only aid in understanding governmental structure if an individual can be helped to see the ways in which it is functioning properly as well as the ways in which it isn't.

There are, of course, other reasons why we need to teach kids about the realities of the function of their government. The first of these is that it would almost certainly reduce the amount of disillusion, disassociation, and alienation that apparently occurs among our populace. Certainly if kids have been shown all along that our governments are not perfect, that the theory isn't always properly translated into practice, and that even bright and honest governmental leaders can make dumb mistakes, the discrepancy between theory and practice will not come as such an alienating shock. Further, such an endeavor should help us to send kids into the adult world with an awareness of those aspects of our systems of government that require improvement. Thus, not only can we reduce the damaging impact of reality, we can also provide an awareness of those things that need to be done to reduce the gap between the theory and practice of democracy. Now I know, and know well, that in advocating the deliberate and continuous examination of political realities, I am pointing teachers in the direction of controversy. What can I say? While I truly believe we are more secure when we worry about doing our job rather than when we are obsessed with trying to keep it, this is small comfort to someone who is reticent about encountering controversy. Actually the only response I can give is yes, this is exactly what I am suggesting. In all candor, I do not see any way in which we will develop responsible citizens and at the same time avoid the potential for considerable controversy. Even though I am going to suggest some things in the final chapter that I trust will increase the feeling of teacher security, this doesn't reduce the possibility that an effective program of citizenship education will generate some heat from some sources. Be this as it may, the task is so important, so crucial, that somehow we must find the courage it will require of us.

Beyond this business of dealing with the realities of the operation of government, there are two other things that I feel will be worthy of inclusion among those things we want our students to know. These are an understanding of other forms of government and a grasp of the philosophical basis of democracy. The major reason for both of these additions is that they may serve to increase the strength and depth of support for the basic tenets of democracy.

In the market place of ideas, democracy doesn't exist in a vacuum apart from other possible forms of government. If one is to really understand democracy, it is necessary to see it in relationship to other possible social arrangements. In saying this, I want to make it clear that I'm talking about honest and open comparison with other possible forms of government. I'm not talking about cheap attempts to propagandize, and stack the deck in favor of democracy over and above other forms of government. More specifically I am not writing in support of the kind of "comparative" effort that was represented by the "Americanism versus Communism" courses that were foisted off on school children by superpatriots during the McCarthy era. If democracy is the superior form of government that we say it is, it can stand honest comparison--warts and all- with any other form of government. If it can't survive this kind of careful and open examination, it's not worth worrying about. So when I advocate comparative examination of various forms of government, I mean just that. Quite frankly I think the end result will be a stronger and deeper understanding of, and commitment to democracy.

Of course what I'm after in advocating a study of the philosophical foundations of democracy (other than the fact that philosophy is my field and I think it important) is the basic ideas about human beings and their relationships that undergird this particular form of government. More specifically I am concerned that every student come to understand that this form of government is dependent on a genuine belief in the worth and dignity of each individual human being. Further, this commitment, requires that human beings have reserved to them certain basic rights. And finally that democracy depends on commitment to a belief in the quality of and the necessity of shared decision-making in the marketplace of competitive ideas. However, it will not be enough for us to succeed in conveying these general ideas--no matter how deeply they may be held--to our students. Beyond this we must help them to see what the application of these basic principles means in a wide variety of specific cases. Only as our charges come to see that democracy requires the uniform application of these basic principles in every case will we have developed the depth of support that democracy demands.

In these new undertakings that I have suggested it will be best whenever possible and practical to approach them from the perspective of current problems. In fact, this approach should undergird all our attempts to develop the knowledge we feel is necessary for responsible citizenship. If we are to succeed in helping kids acquire this knowledge in lasting and usable form, it must be seen by them as having meaning and application in their lives. Our best bet then is to approach these things from the present in terms of current events, current problems, and current application.

THE SKILLS

The first category of necessary citizenship
skills is so obvious that in mentioning them I feel
as though I'm treading on the trite. These skills,
of course, are the techniques of communication. Without the capacity to deal effectively with the sounds
and symbols of social intercourse an individual isn't
going to function very well in many aspects of his life
and certainly not in that portion known as responsible
citizenship. If a person can't read, watch, write,
listen, speak, and cipher, his potential for effective
learning is greatly limited. Thus, the first--and
primary--skills of responsible citizenship are those
of communication.

While there is always room for improvement, I
do not hold with those who contend that the schools
have failed to develop a people who can communicate.
Surely there are those among us who neither read nor
write very well. Certainly we should continue to be
concerned about those with whom we fail. But, in this
matter of skills of communication, we succeed more
than we fail. I have lived now long enough to have
experienced several generations moaning and groaning
over the youngsters "going to hell in a wheelbarrow."
Old coots that gripe about the schools producing
secretaries that can't spell as they did in the good
old days are full of baloney. So far as reading,
writing, and ciphering are concerned, we have never
done as well as we would have liked, nor as poorly as
our critics have claimed. We've never really left the
"basics" that some have raised a hue and cry for us to
go back to.

In this regard, then, I offer two suggestions.
First, we could probably well spend some additional
time in trying to help kids learn to speak and listen
better. (We may have some trouble with this latter as
we teachers don't know a heck of a lot about listening.)
Second--and this is rapidly becoming my recurring
theme--we can make a greater effort to see that the
vehicles we use to help the students develop these

skills consist of material that is of genuine significance to our pupils.

Closely related to the skills of communication
are the skills of information acquisition. (This is
just a fancy label for staying informed.) This is not
particularly complex and simply requires that we demonstrate to our students the means of regularly monitoring several sources of information. It should be
easy to develop such skills through the current events
activities that I suggested in the preceding chapters.

Likewise, teaching the skills that relate to
the mechanics of citizenship is not a complicated undertaking. It only entails making a list of those
skills that a citizen needs to have at his command,
such as how to operate a voting machine and giving the
students experience in each of these functions.

Teaching the remaining skill of citizenship,
critical thinking, is not so easily managed. Even so,
there are several successful approaches to the development of the various skills of critical thinking that
are available. While I'm not going to cover every
detail of each, I do want to deal in some depth with
some of the more promising of these approaches.

When you boil it down, all types of critical
thinking have in common the use of an orderly and
systematic approach to decision making and problem
solving. Most of them take the form we refer to as the
"scientific method." We teachers have generally recognized this fact but haven't done a whole lot about
it. In the main we have contented ourselves with
teaching the scientific method in some science course,
like biology, and assumed that this would result in the
student's being a critical thinker in all areas of his
life. Obviously this has been a false assumption. If
we are to develop citizens who can think critically
about the problems that confront their society, we
must specifically teach them how to think critically
about those kinds of problems.

To begin with, we can teach the kids the various
techniques of propoganda and how to detect their use.
Certainly we can help them learn to recognize the
appeal to the emotions that is the approach that under-
girds all propaganda. Beyond this, we can teach them
to use the propaganda classification system developed
back in 1937 by the Institute of Propaganda Analysis.[1]
This system uses seven categories to classify the

99

techniques of propaganda: name calling, glittering
generality, transfer, testimonial, plain folks, card
stacking, and band wagon. Even though some forty years
have elapsed since this particular system of categories
was developed, it is as applicable today as it was
then. While some of the means of communication have
changed dramatically since 1937, the techniques of
propaganda have not, and youngsters can be taught to
apply this means of analysis in today's world. There
is even a game available, based on this particular
method of propaganda analysis, that can be used in the
classroom to help develop competence in this skill.[2]
However, since the TV advertisments that constantly
bombard the students provide a never-ending parade of
the various techniques of propaganda, it seems to me
that the "tube" is the most promising vehicle for use
in the development of this skill.   (This kind of
approach, of course, goes hand in glove with such
studies as consumer education.)   Since there is no
area of human activity that makes greater use of all
the techniques of propaganda than does the political
campaign, it regularly presents a wonderful opportunity
to develop this critical thinking skill.   In fact,
most aspects of our curriculum contain areas of controversy and emotion that are subject to propagandizing
and present us with limitless opportunities to develop
this skill of propaganda analysis.   (I realize that
the development of students skilled in propaganda de-
tection will present some problems for those of us who
do quite a bit of propagandizing as we teach.   Nonetheless,   I trust the gain will be worth the possible
loss.)

Hugh Rank, writing in the National Council of
Teachers of English book Teaching About Doublespeak,
indicates that he feels the Institute of Propaganda
Analysis techniques are not applicable today.[3]   On
the contrary, he advocates that we teach a schema which
he believes is free of the technical errors found in

---

[1]Propaganda Analysis, 1:2, (1937), Institute of Propaganda Analysis.

[2]Robert W. Allen and L. Green, The Propaganda Game, Box
71 BA, New Haven, Connecticut 06501.

[3]Daniel Dieterich, ed., Teaching About Doublespeak,
"Teaching About Public Persuasion: Rationale and a Schema,"
Urbana, Illinois, National Council of Teachers of English, 1976,
pp. 3-19.

earlier approaches and is better suited for analysis of today's sophisticated communication. Rank, who contends that the old IPA system requires too rigid a treatment of propaganda techniques, proposes in its place a system of identifying propaganda as either "intensification" or "downplay." It is his belief that we--including the propagandists--tend to intensify the good and downplay the bad in those things that we support, and intensify the bad and downplay the good in those things we oppose. Apparently, for Rank there is no real distinction between normal human discourse and deliberate propaganda except possibly the motivation behind it. (And herein lies the weakness of his schema; if everything is, nothing isn't.) According to Rank, the techniques of "intensification," or emphasizing are repetition, association, and composition; and those of "downplay" are omission, diversion, and confusion. While I still think the 1937 system of propaganda analysis is adequate, Rank has developed a workable schema, and those who are interested in teaching propaganda analysis would be well advised to read his work. As for me, I'm concerned that we use some systematic approach to the teaching of propaganda analysis, and which one is of no great concern to me.

In this field of propaganda analysis, the National Council of Teachers of English, through its committee of Public Doublespeak, has recently made outstanding contributions with its books Language and Public Policy and Teaching About Doublespeak.[4] If you are looking for some specific and concrete proposals on how to teach propaganda analysis in the elementary and secondary schools, you will find them in the latter book. (Some of the programs contained in Teaching About Doublespeak are directly related to the use of propaganda in politics.)

Another approach to critical thinking, designed to develop the skills of effective probing, is frequently referred to as inquiry training. The basic idea here is that the method and the material of study are to center around the questions raised by the students. An earlier similar approach--perhaps the earliest--has been labeled the Socratic method after the late, great philosopher of Athens. In essence those who advocate the inquiry method would have teachers

---

[4]Ibid. and Hugh Rank, Language and Public Policy, Urbana, Illinois, National Council of Teachers of English, 1974.

abandon their concern with covering subject matter and help students examine and clarify their own observations and concerns. Thus the subject matter is to be developed through the interest and concerns of the students as they learn to find the answers to questions that are of genuine significance to them. While there are numerous programs that center around the inquiry approach, I recommend the work of Postman and Weingartner in Teaching as a Subversive Activity.[5] Although some of their language is out of the "be gross" era, and some of their proposals are designed for shock effect, their basic approach to the development of this particular skill of critical thinking is a sound one. In particular I am impressed with their recognition of the importance of a teacher attitude and a classroom environment that support a climate in which authentic inquiry can occur.

Based on the work of Hilda Taba, the Institute for Staff Development since 1967 has been actively promoting a program for the development of skills of deductive reasoning in school children.[6] This program, known as the Hilda Taba Teaching Strategies and based on her early work, is a highly structured approach to critical thinking. The activities in the program are designed to teach children the skills of concept development, data interpretation, generalization application, feeling exploration, and conflict resolution. "Development of concepts" is learned through a process of enumerating items from the students' experience, grouping these items on the basis of some similarity, identifying the common characteristics of each group, and assigning labels to them. The specific activities involved in learning the "interpretation of data" are listing of specific data from material studied, searching for causal relationships, drawing inferences, listing prior causes and subsequent effects of inferences arrived at, and drawing conclusions and generalizations. Having arrived at generalizations, students learn their application through a process of making predictions, developing means of support for their predictions, developing bases for determining

---

[5]Neil Postman and David Weingartner, Teaching as a Subversive Activity, New York, Delacorte Press, 1969.

[6]Hilda Taba Teaching Strategies Program, 3000 Biscayne Boulevard, Suite 316, Miami, Florida, 1971. (There are two editions: one for Elementary and one for Secondary teachers. Each edition has four units.)

the plausibility of their predictions, and inferring the consequences of the application of their generalizations. The Taba approach has the potential for wide application, as it is adaptable to almost any subject matter. To learn to use the strategies effectively requires that you receive specific instruction in the application of the techniques. While I consider the tight structure of the program and the need for intensive training deterrents to the widespread use of this program, it is still a technique of teaching that is well worth inclusion in a teacher's repertoire.

In his book, Teaching Critical Thinking,[7] James Drake uses some of the approaches of analytic philosophy in the program that he advocates. As the vehicle for teaching critical thinking, he advocates the use of what he terms "dialogue teaching." In essence this approach is simply open and authentic discussion and inquiry involving the students and teacher. He specifically states that this kind of approach can be used in the development of classroom rules. Further, he feels that teachers should frequently move beyond the process of exploring "facts" and deal with what he terms "meta-issues." Actually "meta-issues" turns out to be dealing with the "why" of various issues--moving beyond the mere listing of information and exploring the causal factors. In this latter part of his work, where he deals with classroom application, Drake is pretty vague and general. This is the major weakness of his program. However, if you understand his basic approach--something that isn't really very difficult to do--you can figure out your own means of application. In any event, it's worth knowing about.

The approach to critical thinking that has been developed by Richard Phillips is much influenced by the philosophy of pragmatism.[8] In fact, his definition of the complete act of thinking is synonymous with the application of the scientific method to a problem. Further, it is Phillips' contention that no critical thinking occurs except as it is elicited by the development of a problem. According to him, until we encounter a problem, we simply move through life operating on a series of unexamined and unquestioned

---

[7]James A. Drake, Teaching Critical Thinking, Danville, Illinois, The Interstate Printers and Publishers, 1976.

[8]Richard C. Phillips, Teaching for Thinking in High School Social Studies, Reading, Massachusettes, 1974.

assumptions.   Thus, if critical thinking is to be
developed, the first task of the teacher is to intro-
duce doubt into the perceptual field of the student,
thus creating a problem. The teacher, having created
a problem, then teaches the student to apply the method
of science, or critical thinking, to its solution. To
facilitate this approach, Phillips advocates the development of a permissive yet rigorous atmosphere in the
classroom. In this atmosphere he would have us teach
the rudiments of both inductive and deductive logic,
and the development of skills in various kinds of
"thinking operations." In connection with this latter
concern, he sets forth specific practices that can be
adopted to help students understand their language
usage. Further, he explains techniques to develop
skills in comparing and contrasting, classifying,
observing and reporting, summarizing, interpreting, an-
alyzing assumptions, and evaluating. While the work
of Phillips is aimed specifically at social studies
teachers, those things to which I have referred can be
easily adopted by teachers in other disciplines. I
suppose the fact that my theoretical orientation is
similar to that of Phillips has a great deal to do with
my appreciation of his basic approach. Even so, there
are parts of his work that appear to be unnecessarily
complicated and frequently his writing is cluttered
with superfluous quotes from various sources. (This
latter problem--excessive name dropping--is, I am
discovering, a great temptation. When I think of the
twin advantages of overwhelming with sources and creating an image of being well-read, I'm hard put to leave
out any documentation that seems even close to being
applicable.) Nonetheless, his chapter entitled 'Developing Thinking Skills in the Social Studies" is full
of specific things that can be done by any teacher to
help kids become more skilled in critical thinking and
is worth the reading.

        The final approach to teaching critical thinking
that I want to describe is part of a program developed
by Matthew Lipman and expanded in collaboration with
him by those in the Institute for the Advancement of
Philosophy for Children.[9]   It is Lipman's central
thesis that philosophical thinking can be taught to
school children. The vehicle through which he seeks to
accomplish this task is what he terms "the philosophical novel." At this writing he and his associates have
completed two such novels--complete with teacher
guides--which, among other things, seek to develop in
children some skills of human thought that I would
label aspects of critical thinking. The two novels,

Harry Stottlemeier's Discovery for fifth and sixth graders and Lisa for seventh and eighth graders, are the first components of what the Institute intends to develop as a comprehensive program of philosophy for school children from kindergarten through the twelfth grade. In these novels, using the language and con-concerns of children, Lipman teaches the basics of both formal and nonformal logic. (For those of us who endured the memorization of sterile rules of logic to be applied to trivia and nonsense, this approach to formal logic will be hard to recognize.) Without ever concerning the students with the various labels, the novels take them through the rules on which consistency, truth preservation, and coherence are based in formal logic. Further, the principles of nonformal logic are set forth, along with some criteria to be used in evaluation of this approach to thinking. Beyond these specific activities for the development of skills of logic, the program promotes what is termed "philosophical discussion," which, with its concern for examination of assumptions, generalizations, implications, and inferences is simply another approach to critical inquiry. I like this program. I like the idea of using a novel as the vehicle for approaching children. And, even though to some sixth graders Harry Stottlemeier may be somewhat of a klutz, I like the idea of dealing with kids on their own terms in connection with problems that at least stand a chance of being real to them. I like the idea that philosophy can be included in the public school classroom and can serve as a means of unifying otherwise compartmentalized studies. I like the reports that Lipman and company cite which indicate that kids who have been through this program show considerable improvement in reading. I also like the idea that these people don't claim that their program will cure all the ills of education--just some of them. And finally, I like the attempts they are making to provide interested teachers and other educators with some training in the use of their program. This leads me

---

[9]Matthew Lipman, A.M. Sharp, F.S. Oscanyan, Philosophy in the Classroom, Upper Monclair, N.H., Montclair State College, The Institute for the Advancement of Philosophy for Children, 1977. In addition to Harry and Lisa mentioned in the text, this group has also produced an Instructional Manual to Accompany Harry Stottlemeier's Discovery. Matthew Lipman has also produced a filmstrip series entitled Thinking About Thinking, which can be secured from Ergo Films, Los Angles, California. Lipman is also co-editor with Ann Margaret Sharp of Growing Up with Philosophy, Philadelphia, Pa., Temple University Press, 1978.

to my major concern with their work. It seems to me that to teach logic you need some depth of understanding of logic (not necessarily the "vacuum variety" I mentioned earlier), some grasp of the structure of philosophy, and a tremendous talent for leading philosophical discussion. Before it's over, it may be determined that this program will require the same sort of rigid structure and intensive training that is used for the Taba strategies.

What I've just worked through is by no means an exhaustive listing of the various programs developed to teach critical thinking, nor was it intended to be. What I've done is list some of the better approaches that are representative of the various means through which teaching of the skills of critical thinking can be accomplished. The main point in my doing this is to demonstrate that there are such programs--that there are those who know how to go about developing these skills.

That so few of us are trained in any of these approaches carries with it a message that should--but probably won't--be loud and clear for the colleges of education. If we ever get serious about developing critical thinkers, it will become incumbent on those institutions that train teachers to show them how to teach it. Surely, even today when we profess to seek to develop critical thinking, it is asinine that the technuqies by which it is taught are ignored (or unknown) in most of the colleges of education.

In addition to the fact that all of the various approaches to critical thought draw heavily on the so-called method of science, they also have in common a concern that a certain kind of atmosphere exist in any classroom in which critical thinking is to be taught. Every one of the programs that I have mentioned in one way or another states that a climate of inquiry--a supportive environment, if you please--must exist. This, then, leads me to the topic of the next chapter. It is my contention that it is not likely that any of the skills we teach will be well learned, or often used, unless they are taught in an environment that really supports their use. It is not enough that we provide kids with information; we must get them to use it. It isn't enough to teach our charges the various skills of citizenship; we must get them to apply them. Unless we can develop the attitudes that enable them to apply the information and use the skills, we have wasted a great deal of our time as well as theirs. Let's turn then to this business of attitudes and to the environments and examples on which they are based.

THE ATTITUDE THROUGH ENVIRONMENT

Let's get one thing straight from the outset:
all teaching involves, in one way or another, the deliberate attempt to change the life of another human
being. This immediately assumes that the teacher has
some goal in mind as he sets about the task of instruction. Whether his goal is to channel or to free
the student, he is in every instance trying to change
him in terms of some system of values. From this perspective, it is easy to see that there is no such
thing as neutral or objective teaching. Every teacher
is trying to inculcate some kind of value structure in
every student. Having recognized this fact, I want
to turn to the means by which I think we can hope to
inculcate into our charges those values that will encourage them to support in depth the basic tenets of
respresentative democracy and to carry out the functions of responsible citizenship.

Most of the evidence with which I am familiar
points to the conclusion that we absorb the bulk of
our values from the environment in which we find ourselves. Further, within our environment, the most influential element in determining our values is the
example of those of importance to us. The psycholo-
gists refer to these individuals as "significant
others." The actions of significant others--the things
we see them value, the things we see them treat as
important--constitute a most potent force in the development of our value structure. If, then, we school
teachers are going to undertake the job of developing
certain values, from which desired attitudes should
follow, it will be necessary that we direct our attention to the environment of our students and to the significant others who inhabit it.

Obviously there is not much we teachers can do
to exercise influence over the "out of school" environment of our students or over the significant others
that people this portion of their world. Perhaps, if
we are successful in creating responsible citizens in
this generation, they, as parents, will make our job

with future generations much easier by being supportive
significant others in the environments of their
children. Be this as it may, there is little, if anything, we can do about the present parents, homes, and
neighborhoods from which our pupils come. It seems to
me that it is as much a waste of time to expend effort
in grandiose "reach the parents" programs as it is to
dissipate our energies through condemning them. For
all intents and purposes, the parents are beyond the
reach of our influence. In the face of this, let's
direct our attention, energies, and actions to that
which we can do something about: the environment of the
school and the example of that significant other called
"teacher."

Most schools as they exist today consist of
environments that are not conducive to the development
of responsible citizens, and in fact are actually detrimental to this. A school environment that teaches
the student that it's OK to talk things to death without ever taking any action is detrimental to the development of the responsible citizen. In like fashion
a school that treats the ancient Egyptians as more
significant than the Arab-Israeli crisis, that treats
sterile bits of information from the yellowed pages as
if they are of greater consequence than the pressing
issues of the day, is not an environment that supports
citizenship development. The same indictment can be
leveled against schools that stifle inquiry, abhor
critical thought, limit and restrict decision making,
and made a farce of democratic self-government.
Further, it is certain that schools that through their
environment convince future citizens that they are
powerless to control their own destinies and that seek
to channel, control, and manipulate every aspect of
the lives of these children cannot possibly produce a
people that are fit to be free. And, friend, if you
will take a look at the schools of our nation, you will
find that, with few exceptions, they do indeed treat
the trivial as though it were important, curb most
efforts to make critical examination, arrive at decisions, and translate those decisions into action, and
make a total mockery of the concepts of individual
freedom and responsible self-government. This school
environment, then, is one of the two major reasons that
the schools have guaranteed that this nation would have
a citizenry that has forgotten most of the citizenship
information it acquired, failed to apply what skills
it may have learned, and developed attitudes that have
insured irresponsible citizenship performance. Let me
hasten to add that I don't think this has occurred as

part of some malicious subversive plot or that it is
the result of the activities of "bad guy" teachers.
Rather, it is the end result of a trap we have fallen
into, that we are probably unaware of, and that will
require tremendous effort to extricate ourselves from.

When most children first arrive at school, they
are illiterate, inexperienced, unsophisticated, and
immature. They are not capable of exercising much
sound judgment and require a great amount of supervision. We teachers, who under the law are responsible
for these children, and who, by virtue of our professional commitment, would feel responsible for their
safety and welfare anyway, undertake the task of seeing
that these children are closely supervised and pro-
tected from the perils of their immaturity. Where
they are, we are. By the little hand we lead them to
the library, the toilet, the playground, the lunchroom,
and the bus. With the very young this is as it should
be. Unfortunately, once this pattern is in operation,
other factors seem to intervene, and we never change
our basic approach to children despite the passage of
twelve long years or more of education and maturation.
So it is that when a student is in high school we
figuratively take him by his, now large hand and, in
the form of hall passes, monitors, and penalities, lead
him around the school house. As I said, there are
several factors that serve to reinforce this pattern
of constant supervision and surveillance that is the
environment of our schools. The first of these is the
idea that we, the teachers, --the adult respresentatives
of society--know what is best for the children. Heck,
more often than not, particularly with the very young,
we do. This, however, doesn't mean that we are always
the ones who are in possession of superior wisdom. In
fact, if we were really this all-knowing, we would know
that it is of vital importance that kids be allowed to
make decisions and make mistakes if they are to make
any real progress in developing self-control. Certainly, as a child develops and matures, we should deliberately and steadily withdraw from our roles as his
decision maker and have him rely more and more on his
own self-determination. This, however, isn't what we
are inclined to do. On the contrary, we educators
continue all the way through the advanced stages of
graduate school to function as though we are the only
ones who know what is good for our students, what they
need to know, and what they must do. Having once committed ourselves to the position of the omniscient
authority--even in the face of steady maturation--we
seem powerless to abandon this indefensible position

even though we succeed in maintaining it only through constant recourse to our authoritarian position.

When you add to this attitude our tenacious clinging to the long-discredited concept of "habituation," you come up with the idea that not only do we know what is best for the children, but also we are obligated to force them to do these "good things." They must study these important things and be drilled in these crucial skills until these essentials are deeply ingrained in their mental fibre. While there may be, in some instances, grounds for our assumption that we know best, there are no substantial grounds to support our continued belief that we can successfully habituate children to do what we and society want done. Yet, we persist in trying and trying and trying.

As if these two factors weren't enough to keep us committed to an "incarceration environment" in our schools--where we feel compelled to know exactly where everyone is and what each one is doing--there is another attitude among far too many of us that further compounds the problem. We don't trust kids. Or, to put it another way, because there are some kids that we can't trust, we have a strong tendency to treat all of our students as though they cannot be trusted. Take a hard look at a set of school rules and you'll see what I mean. Almost without exception we establish our rules in terms of the worst actions of the worst element of our school population. When we do this, we put ourselves in the position of treating the overwhelming majority of our students, who I believe can be trusted, as though they were untrustworthy. Having arrived at this position, we move easily to viewing the student body as a group committed to getting away with things, beating the system, evading the ever-increasing list of rules, and subverting the best efforts of the faculty. Once we start thinking this way, the role of the faculty automatically becomes one of checking, searching, watching, and catching. Ergo, "the student as enemy." If you think this doesn't happen, sit and listen to the talk of your colleagues. Think about your own attitude.

Well, when you put all the above factors together, small wonder we end up with school environments that are so terribly detrimental to the development of responsible citizens. Such environments couldn't be less conducive to our objective if they had been deliberately designed to subvert our efforts. Even recognizing this, we must face the fact that it will not be easy to

111

change this environment as it will require of us that we change our basic approach to youngsters. Because the approach to children that creates our present environment is so deeply ingrained within the system, and within us, it will require monumental efforts on our part if we are to see any meaningful change.

Let's suppose for a while that somehow we teachers manage to reorient ourselves and adopt an approach to students that is more conducive to developing responsible citizens. What will our schools be like?

First, we will establish an environment in our schools in which it is O.K. to make mistakes. Now I don't mean by that that we will abandon our "standards" (whatever these may be) and treat wrong answers as though they were just as correct as right answers or any other equally ridiculous interpretation of "It's O.K. to make mistakes." Rather, I mean that we will establish an atmosphere where it is recognized and accepted that people--including teachers--often make errors. That even teachers don't know everything. That, in fact, the more one learns, the more he recognizes how little he knows. We will establish an environment in which we face up to the reality that on many matters there is no one right answer or correct decision or single course of action. In sum, we will recognize the fallibility of both the student and the teacher and concentrate on methods of inquiry rather than pre-determined answers. The environment will be one of questioning and examining--of honest seeking and searching--in which the teacher is a participant in the process. (Granted, the teacher is, or should be, a far more knowledgeable participant.) Now, I want to be very clear here that I am not advocating some approach in which we pretend that none of us knows anything and that all of us must discover everything. What I am advocating is that each of us recognize that we are all short of being repositories of total knowledge, that we are all involved, at one level or another in the process of inquiry, and that it is necessary that each of us seek his own answers. If we can establish such an atmosphere of open inquiry, we will have made a major contribution to the development of an environment in which the skills of critical thinking can really be used.

In like fashion, we will develop an environment in which the kids are not only permitted to assume responsibility for decision making, but are expected to. It seems to me that it is entirely possible for us to deliberately develop a program in which we open ever-expanding decision-making possibilities to our students. I don't know of a specific program I can refer you to in which this has been done. In fact, I don't know that it _has_ been done anywhere. However, I do know that it _can_ be done. I believe that we know enough about child development that we can design a program in which youngsters are given ever-increasing amounts of responsibility for making decisions, acting on these decisions, _and_ _receiving the_ _consequences of_ _their acts._[1] Obviously, with the very young, the kinds of decisions that could be open to them would be quite limited. There _are_ things that they cannot be permitted to do; there _are_ things they need to learn; and there _are_ judgments that they are not yet capable of making. On the other hand, there are, even at this age, many paths they should be free to choose, many interests they should be able to pursue, many decisions they should be capable of making, many actions they should be permitted to take, and many consequences they can safely encounter. It seems to me that it is possible to develop a whole series of decision-making levels, in which each level would have wider parameters for decision-making than the level which precedes it. If we will apply four criteria to the development of such a program, I see no real reason why we shouldn't meet with success. First, we cannot let children undertake decisions on matters in which one of the options would result in jeopardizing the safety, health, or psychological well-being of anyone. Second, we will include within the decision-making province of each child things that are of real significance and importance to him. Third, we will not pretend to involve students in decision-making when this is not what we are really doing. Fourth, as a child demonstrates the capacity to handle decisions successfully at one level, we will move him to the next level. In all candor, I believe if we will just devote as much effort to the development and implementation of such a program as we now expend on trying to make kids adhere to the decisions we have made for them, we will succeed beyond our fondest dreams. I think we will soon learn that most of our charges are capable of assuming much more responsibility for themselves than we ever imagined and

---

[1] Rudolf Dreikurs in Children: The Challenge, New York, Merideth Press, 1968, advocates a somewhat similar approach in dealing with children. He says it works. However his experience is with parent-child relationships and, as far as I know, his approach has not been tried in a school setting.

that they are capable of developing into young adults who can make reasonable and rational decisions. (I wish I could outline some specific program through which this progressive development of decision-making could be implemented, but I don't have one. I do hope that because I have only devoted a couple of paragraphs to it you won't get the idea that I think it unimportant. On the contrary, I think it one of the most vital and significant suggestions I have to make.)

As we go about developing a school environment that is conducive to responsible citizenship, it will be necessary that we take great care to avoid doing anything that makes a farce out of democracy. Let's make absolutely certain that when we say we are involving students in decision-making that this is what we are actually doing. Let's stay as far away as we possibly can from such shams as "input," "participation," and "consulting," when we try to involve children in the decision-making process. Under no circumstances should we convey to them that they are being involved in decision-making when in fact they are being manipulated and actually are only being given the opportunity to agree with decisions that have already been made. If we can't really involve them in significant ways, let's don't make any pretense of doing it. In particular we need to exercise great care in what we present to them as "self-government."

If we will take a hard and critical look at our student governments and student councils--organizations that we tell the kids represent their self-government-- we will find that, more often than not, they make a farce of democracy. Most often the reality of student government is that we have the kids elect their representatives, establish their rules and procedures, and deal with anything they want to, so long as they restrict their concerns to matters that are of no importance. We let the student council make such momentious decisions as who will sponsor the next school dance. We let them decide to agree with the principal that it is time for the council to conduct another "clean up the school grounds" campaign. We let them argue and debate about the problems of entering a float in the homecoming parade. But we don't let them deal with anything of real significance. To insure that they don't get beyond the pale, we have a sponsor ride herd on them. And, should this fail, the principal can stop them dead in their tracks by the lifting of a little finger. Whatever this type of student government may represent, it most certainly does not

114

represent self-government and it is not democracy.
True, there is some value to having served on the student council: you can list one more activity beside
your name in the yearbook. Aside from this, student
government, as it is most frequently practiced in our
public schools, is destructive of democracy. Small
wonder that we have produced a citizenry who in large
numbers think that self-government is a sham. Look
at the experience they had in school with "self-
government."

        Several years ago, when I was at Cocoa Beach
High School in Florida, we tried hard to avoid presenting self-government to our students in a form that
would make a mockery of it. We were a new school and
started the year committed to the idea that if we
were unable to develop with the students a means of
self-government that would be credible, we would have
no student government at all. We started the year by
having each social studies class undertake a unit on
self-government. From these classes there emerged a
constitutional convention that undertook the development of a meaningful student government for the school.
As these students worked on this project, it soon
became evident to them that if they were to have a role
of any consequence they would somehow have to get
plugged into the policy-making process of the school.
At this point, they altered the direction of their
efforts and began to work on the development of a
constitution for the whole school. What they finally
produced was a school government that consisted of
three houses: a student government, which had reserved
to it certain matters that were of student concern; a
faculty, which had certain matters that were of teacher
concern reserved to it; and a senate--composed of an
equal number of elected teachers and students--that
was the policy-making body of the school. The administrative head of the school had the power of veto but
the constitution provided a means by which this could
be overridden. Both the students and the faculty
ratified the document. The administration committed
itself to the document, and the government of the
school was organized according to this constitution.
(At this point I want to note the obvious: i.e.,the
school did not exist in a vacuum. All involved recognized this. It was well understood that the school
would have to function within the structure of state
statute and school board regulations. To conform to
this reality, the constution made provision for an
attorney general, who was to interpret the constitution
and review all proposals to make sure that they were

not contrary to state law or school board regulartion.)
The constitution wasn't perfect and the organization
that developed from it was not without its faults. In
the early stages of its implementation the plan lacked
credibility with the kids and many of them thought that
we were just going through a more elaborate method of
playing the same old game. Likewise there were some
trying moments when the administration found itself in
the position of implementing some senate-developed policies that left much to be desired. Despite these
times of trial, the school continued to operate and, as
the full meaning of the system became increasingly evident, its effectiveness improved. All of that to say
this: on its worst day it was not a failure and it
improved with time. And even on its worst day it was
real self-government. It was not an easy undertaking,
and on each day it required a strong commitment from
both the administration and the faculty. I would hazard
a guess that unless that strong commitment has been
maintained you would be unable to find even the slight-
est vestige of that brief shining moment at Cocoa Beach
High School today. I haven't been back to take a look.
I tell you about this particular undertaking to establish the fact that authentic self-government can be
achieved; I've seen it done. If, in our particular
situation, we teachers cannot undertake self-government
of this magnitude, as a poor second we can at least
make very clear to the students the limits within
which they can operate in the name of "student
government." Further, if the area of decision-making
we reserve to them is to be limited to the trivial and
inconsequential, let's make sure they understand that
this is not self-government and not democracy.

    I think the American judicial system has been--
without having this particular goal in mind--helping us
to develop one aspect of the school environment in
order to make it more compatible with the production of
responsible citizens. I am referring to the decisions
about students' rights that have come from the courts
of late. For many, many years under the principle of
in loco parentis (in place of the parent) the only
right a student had was protection from cruel and un-
usual punishment. Even this minimal right was not
universally available and existed in writing more often
than it existed in practice. However, in more recent
years the courts have made the discovery that school
children are, in fact, small American citizens. There
has been a general--though fluctuating--trend toward
giving these "citizens" the full protection of constitutional rights. While I realize that this has

brought groans of anguish from the less secure and talented among our professional brethren, it is none-theless a trend toward an environment that is more supportive of citizen development. We should do all we can to hasten the fruition of this trend so that kids will learn first-hand that the rights of the constitution are truly available to all American citizens.

Finally, we should create an environment in our schools that encourages kids to move beyond the art-ifical problems of the classroom and deal with the real problems of their world. Not only should we encourage this attitude, we should provide opportunities--many of them--for kids to do this. The world of school child-ren of all ages is filled with real problems on which they can work. Far better to have our "problems in American democracy" classes working to solve some of these problems than to have them merely sitting in class talking about them. However, in writing that last sentence I most certainly don't want to imply that I think this activity should be restricted to the social studies in the upper grades. While I'm going to cite a few examples of some of the more extensive un-dertakings in which students have been involved direct-ly in community problem-solving, much of this kind of activity can be done on a scale less grand. In fact the important factor in this approach is the attitude that supports it, establishes that it is high priority, and that allots time to it. The particular form this approach takes must vary with circumstances. Whether it is first-graders organizing to meet with the princi-pal about better lunchroom food, or third-graders developing a newspaper recycling program, or fifth-graders taking photos of pollution examples and dis-playing them on a map at the local mall, or seventh-graders conducting a letter-writing campaign in favor of a bill to ban throw-away bottles, or a group of ninth-graders establishing a human relations forum to try to reduce community racial relations problems, or a group of eleventh-graders appearing before the school board to request a policy change, the supporting attitude and environment are the same. And the beauty of this is that these kinds of activities will tend to spring naturally from student interest and class-room activities if only the environment that supports them is present.

A very promising though highly structured ap-proach to involving older students in the solution of community problems is the "Skill in Citizen Action"

program.[2] It is designed as an English-Social Studies
program for eleventh and twelfth grade students.
Under the provisions of this program the students would
spend the bulk of one school year learning the communication and social action skills of citizenship
through a combination of classroom and direct application activities. (During this year they would concentrate on this program and would be able to take
only one additional subject.) The classroom activities
would include the political-legal process, communication, and action in literature. The "direct application" aspect of the program would consist of a community service internship and a citizen action project.
This latter activity would also involve the development of a public message through which the students
would interpret the meaning and significance of their
"Skills in Citizen Action" experience.

An example of a massive community action project that
emerged from classroom activity can be seen in a film
entitled Democracy: Your Voice Heard.[3] This film is
an account of the work of the English class of
teacher Bob Donaldson of Denby High School in Detroit.
As a result of their study of The Republic of Plato
the class began to investigate means by which improvement could be achieved in society. The outcome of
this study was the development of a campaign to improve
the conditions of Detroit's Receiving Hospital. This
campaign spread to other schools and to the community
at large. The outcome was the allocation of substantial funds by the city fathers which resulted in dramatic improvements in the hospital. All, according to
those who report this incident, was due to the efforts
of these students. In an English class, yet!

My final example comes from Daviess County High
School in Owensboro, Kentucky.[4] It is of a problems
class that really deals with problems--community problems. Each year the students who elect the course,

[2]Fred M. Newmann, T.A. Bertocci, R. M. Landsness, Skills
in Citizen Action, Madison, Wisconsin, University of Wisconsin
Publication, 1977.

[3]Bob Donaldson, Democracy: Your Voice Heard, Chicago,
Illinois, Coronet Films.

[4]Bill Cox, "Daviess Students Tackle City and County
Problems," Louisville Courier-Journal, Louisville, Kentucky,
May 1, 1972.

"Problems of American Democracy," and are admitted,
work on some problem in the community. The problem
may range from misuse of city cars by councilmen,
through pollution of the Ohio River, to the condition
of downtown Owensboro. The students go through the
structured process of identifying the problem, gather-
ing relevant data, reaching conclusions, proposing
solutions, and developing and implementing programs to
solve the problem. Sometimes they achieve their goal,
sometimes they don't, and it is not uncommon for them
to get into hot water. But they always learn, and this
is the real value of the approach.

Whether the students succeed or fail in any or
all of their attempts to resolve problems within their
society, they learn citizenship skills. They learn
the realities of trying to bring about change in
society. They learn from both their successes and
failures how to go about the process. They learn from
their successes that much can be accomplished through
even a few people working together, and they stand
a much-improved chance of retaining the things they
learn in this fashion. Most importantly they learn
from actual experience that this activity is a right
and an obligation of responsible citizenship. About
all it takes is an environment that will support such
activity and teachers who will allot time for it.

So much for examples of things that can be done
to change the environments of our schools. These are
just examples. What we really need to do is to come
to a good understanding of what constitutes "good"
citizenship in our democracy, take a hard comprehensive
look at the environment of our schools, and change the
environment so that it supports the development of the
attitudes of good citizens rather than detracts from
them. It won't be easy, but it can be done.

THE ATTITUDE THROUGH EXAMPLE

Let's turn our attention now to the matter of
the influence of the "significant others" I mentioned
earlier. More specifically, let's talk about the
example of school teachers, who, in the lives of a
frighteningly large number of school children, loom
as super-significant others. In saying this, I am
aware of the thinking of some that teachers exert
little or no influence on their charges. I think this
belief is a crock. True, some teachers are of little
influence, and no teacher exerts significant influence
on all students. Nonetheless, I've seen far too many
teachers become models for student behavior to agree
with those who tend to discount this aspect of teaching.
Far too many former students have given testimony to
the impact of teachers on their lives to permit us to
consider this as unimportant. At any time, the example of a teacher has the awesome potential of directly influencing the attitude and life of some student.
This being the case, the example of teachers in the
matter of responsible citizenship has the potential to
be of considerable impact--for good or bad--on our
future citizens.

I suppose the obvious thing to say at this point
is that teachers should set a good example for future
citizens by being responsible citizens themselves.
Obviously, yes, but also very true. There are, of
course, other things we can and should do to improve
the caliber of the citizenry we produce. None, however,
is more important than this matter of teacher example.
It is vital that we come to understand that the production of responsible citizens is truly the obligation
of every teacher and that the example of each teacher
is a crucial factor in this process. Perhaps the
colleges of education, if they have any impact at all
on future teachers, can help in this process. They
can at least make the effort to see that their graduates have been told that this is one of the obligations they assume as teachers. Perhaps they can go
even further and undertake to see that prospective
teachers are introduced to the workings of government

and the skills of critical thinking. Perhaps. Actually
I'm more optimistic about the possibility that we
teachers will, on our own, come to understand the crucial importance of our mission in citizenship development and take it upon ourselves to see that we practice
good citizenship. In any event we need to demonstrate
consistently to our charges that we do understand, subscribe to, and practice the basic tenets of democracy.
Further, we need to show them that we understand, subscribe to, and practice the activities of responsible
citizenship. This will fulfill the very minimum requirements of our obligation to provide a positive
example.

Beyond these minimal things, it would really be
good if teachers became so active in their citizenship
role that they assumed positions of real citizen
leadership. It would be a really good example for
youngsters if they saw large numbers of their teachers
involved in politics as active campaigners and as
candidates for office. (Properly done, massive involvement of teachers in the political arena would
likely do much to clean up the process, and could well
result in much-needed increases in the financial
support of education.)

I'm well aware that for the past several years
efforts have been made by the several organizations of
teachers to get educators heavily involved in politics;
there has been some progress. Unfortunately, the results of these efforts have been so clouded with the
puffery of propaganda and ludicrous claims of dramatic
success that the entire movement consists of more sound
than substance. Sigh. Even so, I still have hope that
we may yet learn to avoid the continual reinvention of
the wheel, and get about the business of developing
genuinely workable means of political effectiveness.
We really need to do this because it will result in
better schools, because we can supply a breath of fresh
air to the process, and most of all, because we will
set a good example for the kids.

Since I've referred to "proper" involvement in
the political process, I want to take a little time
to elaborate on this concept. To begin with, my idea
of "proper" means that teachers should work only for
those candidates that they feel are really worthy of
support. I know of some teacher groups that feel they
have developed a sophisticated approach to politics by
trying to ascertain who will win a particular race and
then endorsing that candidate. To begin with,

this approach isn't sophisticated; it's stupid. Even
the most dense politician can see through such a
transparent ploy. But, of even more importance, it's
wrong. We should even avoid the practice of deciding
to support the lesser of two evils. If there isn't a
candidate in a particular race that is really worthy
of our support, we should stay out of that race. Even
better, we should locate and motivate a person of high
caliber to get into the race.

I recall that years ago when I first became a
lobbyist for teachers, one of the veteran teacher representatives urged me to really play up to a particular state senator. I was quite dismayed because I knew
this particular legislator to be an unsavory lush and
lecher who used his senatorial position primarily for
the purpose of personal gain. My response was, "Howard,
he's nothing but an S.O.B." To which he responded,
"Yes, but he's one of our S.O.B's." This approach is
not the kind of example that teachers should set for
school children. People who contend that this is the
only realistic approach that can be taken to politics
don't understand politics and don't understand the
crucial nature of teacher example in this activity.
(Oh, by the way, I dind't play up to the S.O.B.)

Beyond this matter of principle, we need to recognize that only certain political tactics should be
used by teachers and that, further, some tactics won't
work for us. The kinds of tactics that we should never
use are obvious and can all be lumped under the heading
of "dirty tricks." The kinds of tactics that won't
work for us are thoes of high visibility. It has been
my experience that those who are really successful in
politics are not much inclined to make a great deal of
noise about it. If you'ye got it, those who need to,
know it, and there is no need to flaunt it. On the
other hand, if you don't have it, all the talk in the
world won't convince anyone who really makes any difference. The teacher organization's inflated claims
of great political success are ludicrous to anyone who
has any real grasp of politics. In fact, even the
procedure of teacher endorsement is, in my judgement,
highly questionable. The fact that a teacher organization publicly endorses a particular candidate is
not likely to influence any teacher to vote for that
candidate any more effectively than would quietly passing the word through internal communications. And, to
think that teacher endorsement will get a candidate
support from the general public reflects blind ignorance
of the attitudes of the public. There is little reason

122

to think that there is a great reservoir of good will toward teachers among the general public, and there is much evidence that there is little substantial support for public education among this body. Furthermore, it is very likely that there is much latent--if not active --hostility toward schoolteachers at large in the land. Rather than an asset, an endorsement from teachers could well be the kiss of death for a candidate. All in all, if we're serious about developing political effectiveness, we would do well to stop all the brassy press agentry and get about the business of doing well in politics that which we can best do.

While I believe that it is important for teachers to make financial contributions to selected political campaigns, I don't think this is the aspect of politics through which we can expect to achieve much success. We just don't have available to us the kind of financial resources that can make much of a dent in the political process. We should view the financial contributions we make as good faith tokens of the sincerity of our commitment rather than an influential means of political participation. Money just isn't our forte. What we do have that has potential value to a candidate is large numbers of people. There are just a whole lot of school teachers. Now, I'm not talking about the potential of block voting as I view this as unrealistic and undesirable in today's world, particularly among teachers. What I am talking about is campaign workers--a contribution that politicians need and appreciate as much as financial support. This is the area in which our potential strength lies, to provide substantial numbers of people to do the work of the campaigns. And, this--in addition to furthering the cause of good schools and a great profession--could be the very best example we could set for kids: to allow them to see us at work, hard at work, in behalf of those candidates who are truly worthy of our support.

The final aspect of teacher example that I want to deal with involves the operation of the schools themselves. Doesn't it strike you as a little strange that the institution that society has established to develop citizens for our democracy--the public school-- is among the most undemocratic institutions that you can call to mind? What kind of example is this? Democracy isn't practiced in the operation of the public schools of America. On the contrary, the legal structure for the governance of the schools establishes a system that is completely authoritarian. Further, in actual practice the organization and operation of the

public schools of America. On the contrary, the legal
structure for the governance of the schools establishes
a system that is completely authoritarian. Further,
in actual practice the organization and operation of
the schools is as undemocratic as the legal structure
implies. Even such minimal quasi democratic practices
as involving teachers in the decision-making process
is more often than not a sham. Where is the teacher
among us who hasn't experienced manipulation in the
guise of involvement? With disgusting frequency we are
asked for, or permitted to supply, "input" for decisions that will be made by someone else, somewhere else.
Common is the practice of allowing teachers to meet
and agree with a decision that has already been made.
Small wonder that teachers have such a callous attitude
about committee work. Small wonder that teachers give
so little careful attention to the group decisions and
recommendations they make; they know full well that
what they decide, what they recommend, doesn't make any
difference. The truth of the matter is that the administration of the schools is authoritarian from top
to bottom. And, it is we teachers that are the bottom.
What an example!

If this business of democracy is so red hot, if
it is really as good as we tell the students, if it is
really a workable and viable system of governance, why
isn't it used in the schools? After all, here we have
this institution established to convince kids that
democracy is a great system of government; yet we don't
use that great system in this institution. Just how
persuasive can that example be? If it's so great, why
won't it work in the schools?

The fact of the matter is that it will work in
the schools.

Now, friends, hear me out on this if you will.
What I'm about to advocate is foreign to all of your
past experience. To see its full potential will
require of you that you really reorient your thinking.
So, please, before you reject it out of hand, hear me
out and give the idea some serious thought. It really
could be done. Really.

What I'm going to suggest to you is that we re-
organize our schools in such a fashion as to have them
function in a more democratic manner. Obviously, this
would require change in the legal structure of the
school system. This, however, isn't impossible. Contrary to popular myth, the school laws were not

brought down from Mount Sinai on stone tablets. They
can be changed. Furthermore, the conditions that existed at the time these laws were written--and which
no doubt influenced the form they took--have long
ceased to exist. At the time public school law was
originally written, in most cases, the schools were
staffed by many young, (some very young), poorly pre-
pared high school and normal school graduates. These
people required a great deal of supervision and direction. Perhaps, under those circumstances there was
some justification for establishing such a thorough-
going system of authoritarian governance. Today,
however, this is not the kind of person who occupies
our classrooms. On the contrary, today's teacher is
mature and well prepared--an individual who has at
least a bachelors, and in many instances, a master's
degree. Yet the legal structure of another day per-
sists. It can be changed. It should be changed.

What we need to do is set up our schools, all of
them, as semiautonomous democracies. By "semi-auto-
nomous" I mean that these schools would not exist in a
vacuum, but would function as democracies within the
framework of district policy, state statues, and
federal regulation   (I'll deal with this in a little
more detail a little later.)

Under this approach, we would place all of the
decision-making power regarding the operation of a
specific school in the hands of the faculty of that
school. (If, as suggested in the preceding chapter,
under some circumstances the faculty saw fit to share
this power with the students, great.) This, obviously
would mean that the school would no longer have the
need of an administrative head--or principal--at least,
not as we presently know him. (I have found that this
idea seldom elicits enthusiastic response from school
administrators, and on occasion, has precipitated
expressions of downright hostility.) The faculty of
each school would, through the democratic process, establish the operating policies of that school; determine the curriculum; allocate the funds; employ, eval-
uate, and retain or dismiss the personnel; assign loads;
and assume responsiblity for the quality of the operation of that school. Of course this would entail the
extensive use of teacher committees and would require
substantial amounts of teacher time. (It , of course,
takes more time to decide what to do than it takes to
be told what to do.) In all likelihood the faculty
would want to elect a chairperson who would coordinate
the overall operation of the school. This chair could

serve a fixed term with provision for the faculty to remove him for cause. The faculty could provide this chair with such employed help as would make for an efficient school operation. In this regard faculties might want to employ business managers to handle this aspect of the school operation. (Under our present system this is an area of responsibility that frequently demands and receives large allocations of administrator time--an aspect of school administration for which most principals are poorly equipped by both background and training.) Of course the details of operation would necessarily vary from school to school. Think for a minute about schools with which you are familiar. I'm willing to bet that you will begin to see the possibilities, and, without too much effort, figure out the details of how the overall principle I've been discussing could be made to work in those schools. I'm fairly confident that if you can adjust to the basic idea, you can see without much difficulty the mechanics of how teachers can assume responsiblity for policy development and major administrative decisions in any particular school situation.

No doubt at this point it has occurred to you that you know teachers--perhaps many teachers--who wouldn't want to work at something like this and would prefer to continue to have someone else make the decisions for them. I know some of these too. In all likelihood, the poor quality of some of the decisions you have seen teachers make has also come to your mind. I too am aware of some of these bum decisions. I have no pat answer for these, very legitimate concerns. It's my belief--I feel this is more than just wishful thinking--that these conditions are the result of our present system of operation rather than the cause. I think that if teachers became convinced that they were playing for real these conditions would be reduced to negligible concerns. I've seen teachers at work when they knew that the decisions they made would be the action that would actually be taken. On these occasions I have witnessed a willingness to work and work hard, a willingness to assume responsibility, and have seen high quality decisions that have resulted. Even so, I'm sure we would still have some teachers who would long for the good old days because they really prefer to have someone else tell them what to do. And some teachers would continue to make dumb decisions because some teachers are dumb, but I truly believe that we would be pleasantly suprised at how small these numbers would be.

126

It probably has also occurred to you that a democratic system of school governance would serve as an invitation to teachers to play internal politics. Of course it would. So does the present system of governance. In this regard, the main difference that would result from the change to democratic from autocratic, would be to involve all of the teachers in the political process rather than a few.

Within the larger framework of district, state, and nation it is also possible that teachers can be influential. As the practice of collective bargaining increases, teachers, through their democratic organizations, can play a substantial role in the decision-making at the district level. We may well find at the district level that we nave no real need for superintendents as we now know them. Perhaps we could develop this position into some sort of coordinating activity and, as with the individual schools, employ a business manager to handle the business operation. Certainly there is nothing in the proposal that would prevent our having, at the district level, coordinators of subject matter and special concerns. The only difference would be that these individuals would greatly expand the service aspects of their work and reduce to zero their administrative and supervisory activities.

It is possible, even probable, that some will view this suggestion for the operation of school districts as an encroachment on the right of the people to have the final say in the operation of their schools. However, this "final say" of the people has been eroded far more than most of us realize. The concept of local control of schools today is largely a myth. There is nothing in my proposal that would further erode it and might even result in some reversal of this trend. Further, there is nothing in this proposal that would remove the local school board from the picture. Actually, many studies have shown that school boards are seldom representative of the majority or even a good cross-section of the people. Even so, whomever they represent, they would still be there in a policy-making role. What this whole proposal would do is transfer the administrative decision-making power to the local school where the teachers are much more likely to have direct contact with the patrons and where the parents have much easier access. Further it would obviously change the means by which decisions are made at that level. Shoot, it might even be that some schools would want to work out some joint teacher-parent form of democratic governance. Why not? In any

127

event, this move will not result in the control of the schools being further removed from the people.

In the matter of state laws and federal regulations, teachers can again through their democratic organizations participate in political activity, lobbying, and negotiations in behalf of the schools. (Don't think for a minute that state legislatures and the federal congress can't be negotiated with.) Even at these more remote levels of government, teachers, particularly as they learn to function effectively in the political area, can participate in the decision-making process.

What I'm suggesting, then, is that we change the basis of school governance from autocratic to democratic. I think it can be done. I think it can be made to work. Actually, other than the threat it no doubt represents for some persons in positions of authority, there is little to lose and much to gain in trying it. For instance, it would in many situations be most difficult for teachers to make decisions that would be poorer than those that are presently being made. To think otherwise requires that one ignore completely the caliber of some of our school administrators and be blind to some of the incompetent decisions that occur daily within our school systems. Beyond this, there is very much benefit that it could achieve. I am certain that it would result in the development of a profession of teaching that is much more mature and responsible than anything we have ever known. I am fairly confident that it would result in better schools and better education for our children. But, above all else, I am positive that it would set an example that would have great positive impact on our students. For what it would say to them is that we--and through us, society--really believe in democracy. We even believe in it enough to practice it.

So much for the example of the super-significant others.

REALITY

I really hope that through the preceding pages I have done an effective job of persuading you that the production of responsible citizens is the job of public education, that to this point those of us in public education have done a miserable job in this task, but that there are things that, if we did them, would hold promise of turning this failure into success. I hope that I have managed to persuade you that it is of vital importance that we begin at once to produce these responsible citizens. The concept of democracy is too good to be permitted to fall short of its promise or, even worse, to fail. And, though I'm really not one of the prophets of doom, there is no guarantee anywhere that the American government will automatically continue to exist. It is time that we get on with the business of meeting our obligation.

But.

But, how can we?

I started teaching in 1950. That's a while back. My father before me was a teacher. I've known schools and teachers all of my life. I know what they are like. Here I am in the face of all this suggesting that teachers--teachers--bring about dramatic changes in the curriculum, environment, and organization of schools. Further, I'm saying that unless teachers--teachers--do it, it won't get done. Is it realistic to suggest that teachers will do this? Is it realistic to suggest that teachers even can do this? Under the present circumstances, with schools as we know them, and teachers as we know them, the answer is probably not. Fat chance.

But.

But, things have been changing among teachers.

It is in this process of change that my hope resides.

Since the early 1910's there has been a slow
but steady trend in the teaching profession toward the
development of a more mature vocation. This is just
another way of saying the teaching profession has been
growing up. With this progress has come a steady increase in the security teachers feel and an increasing
insistence that they really be involved in the decision-making process. Neither of these trends has
reached proportions of great magnitude, but there is no
question that they exist. This process of maturation
is due in part to the widespread enactment of tenure
laws which have, to some extent, provided teachers with
a measure of security by freeing them from the more
obvious kinds of arbitrary and capricious behavior of
school administrators and school boards. In addition,
the professional standards movement, which has resulted
in the general upgrading of teacher preparation and
performance, has contributed to increased vocational
maturation. But the most significant contribution
to this trend has come as a result of the ever-increasing effectiveness of the professional associations. This
is not to say that the associations of teachers have
even remotely approached their potential. On the
contrary, compared to the effectiveness that teacher
organizations could develop, the progress made to date
is slight. Even so, the slight strength that teacher
associations have developed to this point has opened
up areas of freedom that teachers of another day would
never have dreamed possible. As this freedom has
developed, and as teacher security has increased,
teachers have been willing and able to assume greater
responsibility for the conduct of their own affairs.
Now, please understand that I'm talking about a relative amount of progress. Teachers still don't exercise
a great amount of control over their own destiny, just
a greater amount than in days gone by.

As we have learned how to capitalize on our one
big asset, our large numbers, we have been able to
develop some degree of security and autonomy. What
this really means is that we have within our grasp the
potential to create the conditions under which it will
be possible to change our schools to the kind that will
produce responsible citizens. It's simply a case of
our learning how to better use our great numbers
through our organizations so as to make the association
more effective on our behalf and in behalf of the
school children. I know it can be done, because on
occasion I have seen it done. I've seen it done over
extended periods of time with a relatively small number
of teachers, and I have seen it done for a short period

of time with large numbers of teachers. What I haven't witnessed is this kind of effectiveness generated by large numbers of teachers over a long period of time. But it can be done. I know it can be done. And when it's done, teachers will have the security that will free them to create the schools that ought to be.

If our teacher organizations are soon to become effective enough to really free teachers, there are several things that must be done. To begin with, we need to quit fighting one another. The constant battle for members that goes on between the NEA and AFT, with the accompanying questionable tactics, is a continual drain on our resources. Such activity only tends to confirm the statement of a long-time teacher leader who says, "In time of crisis, you can always count on members of the teaching profession to choose up sides and fight one another." We are not strong enough to be able to expend any energy on internal strife and still achieve any effectiveness. It is long past time for the leaders of these organizations to lay aside their personal ambitions and need for power and to get about the business of looking after the needs and concerns of teachers. And among the chief needs is the need to stop this intraprofessional feuding and develop one comprehensive organization of teachers.

Next we need to develop within the organization of the profession a much more adequate means of two-way communication. In these days of electronics there is no reason why rapid and comprehensive means cannot be developed for wide dissemination of information and rapid grass roots response to it. At any level within the organization it should be possible and practical to keep the membership well informed about issues confronting teachers and decisions that need to be made. By the same token, leaders can have direct access to the attitudes, opinions and recommendations of their entire membership. Such direct involvement in the decision-making process could only serve to strengthen the commitment of teachers to the programs and activities of their organization.

I have already discussed in some detail, in another context, the need for teacher organizations to develop sound means of political involvement. I have little to add here, except to say again that it needs doing and doing in a proper fashion. The teaching profession also needs to continue its concerted effort to obtain collective bargaining throughout the nation. It is through this means, and in my judgement, only

131

through this means, that teachers can really be involved in the decision-making process of a school
district, prior to the decisions being made.

Next, teacher organizations must become more
active in the protection of teachers' rights. While
much progress has been made in this regard, there is
still much left to be done. Every teacher should be
able to approach each day's work secure in the certainty that his profession stands immediately ready to
protect his rights. Even if he is wrong, he should
know that his association will see that he is afforded
all of the protections of due process. And, if he is
right, he needs to be sure that his organization will
fight, bleed, and die for him. Each member of every
school board and all school administrators should know
beyond question that those things they do had best be
legal and ethical or they will answer for their actions
before the bar. I know of no other single thing that
could do more to improve the morale and security for
teachers than the knowledge that they were free of the
petty, arbitrary,and capricious activities of boards
and administrators that have so long plagued our
vocation.

Finally, we need to use our organizations to
assume responsibility for the quality of our performance. You know as well as I that we have among our
numbers those who are unable and/or unfit to teach.
What you perhaps don't know is the terrible price we
have to pay for permitting them to remain in our ranks.
I can assure you that these individuals play a large
role in creating the problems we have of inadequate
school finance and public mistrust. They are a serious
liability to us and we need to be rid of them. It is
not enough for us to say that the administrators should
do their job and clean up the house. These people are
also our responsibility, not because of the harm they
do us but because of the damage they do children.
Through means such as the professional practices com-
missions we need to assume responsiblity for the development of standards of admission to practice, standards
of professional and ethical performance, and the means
for removing--with full due process--those who do not
measure up.

In none of these things that I have just listed
will it be necessary that we start from square one. In
each of them work has been and is being done. What
we need to do is make a strong effort to bring these
movements to rapid fruition. As we achieve these goals,

we will develop a professional organization that is
truly effective and which will serve as the means by
which we obtain the freedom and security necessary
for us to accomplish meaningful change in our schools.
The development of an organization of this level of
effectiveness isn't some pipe dream. It can be done,
and it needs to be done soon. As we accomplish this,
we also need to get about the business of developing
schools that will produce a people truly fit to be
free.